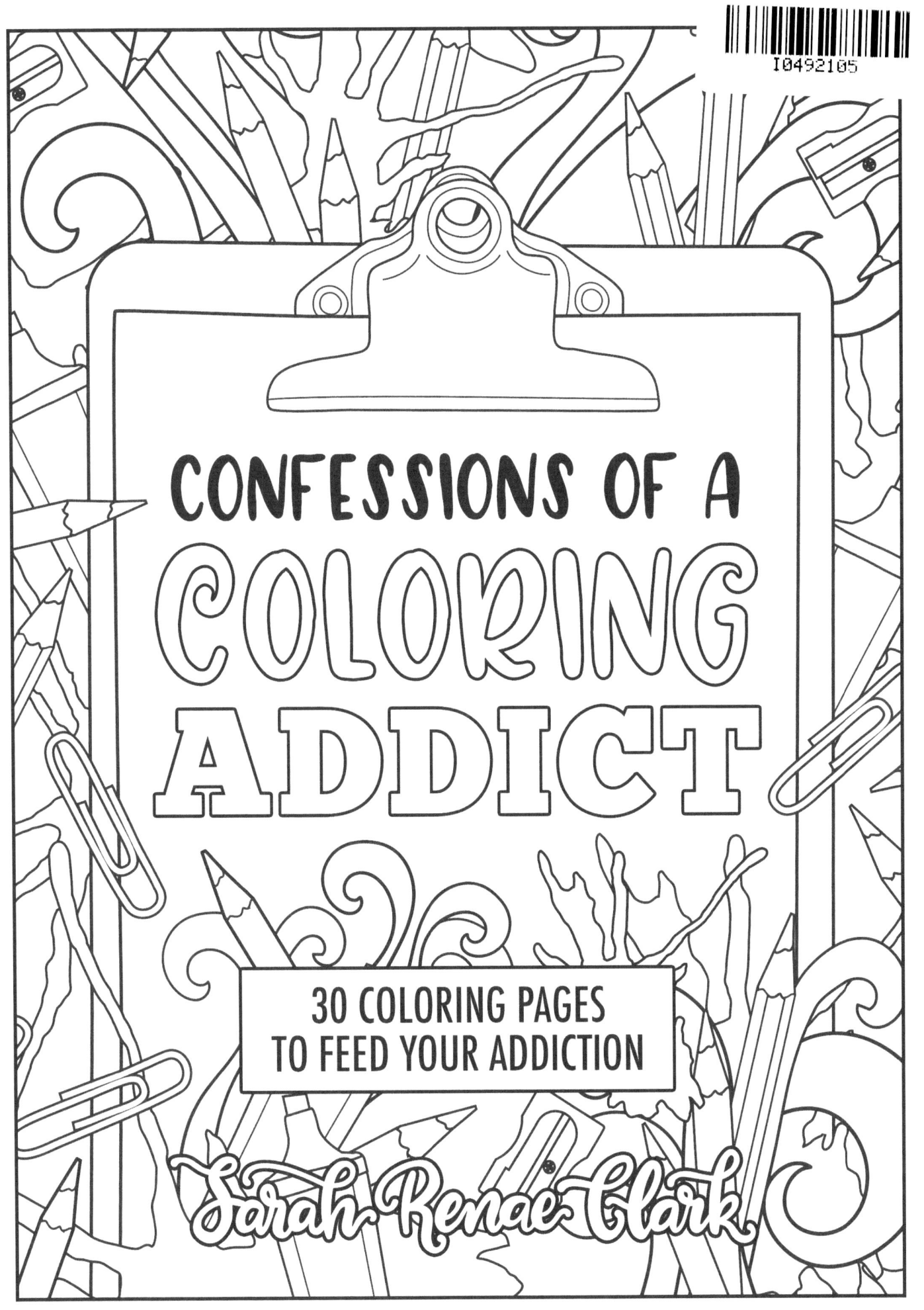

ISBN: 978-1722245238

GENERAL:
All designs in this book are for personal use only. You are welcome to share or post your *personal colored versions only* on social media as long as you attribute Sarah Renae Clark as the artist. Use #sarahrenaeclark to connect with others who are coloring this book.

ARTWORK CREDIT:
All pages and cover were illustrated by Sarah Renae Clark.
Back cover images colored by Linda Franklin, Sarah Renae Clark, Anna Weaver Hurtt, Emma Turnbull and Michelle Huntley Herrema.

For more coloring books, free printables, tutorials and coloring resources, visit:
www.SarahRenaeClark.com

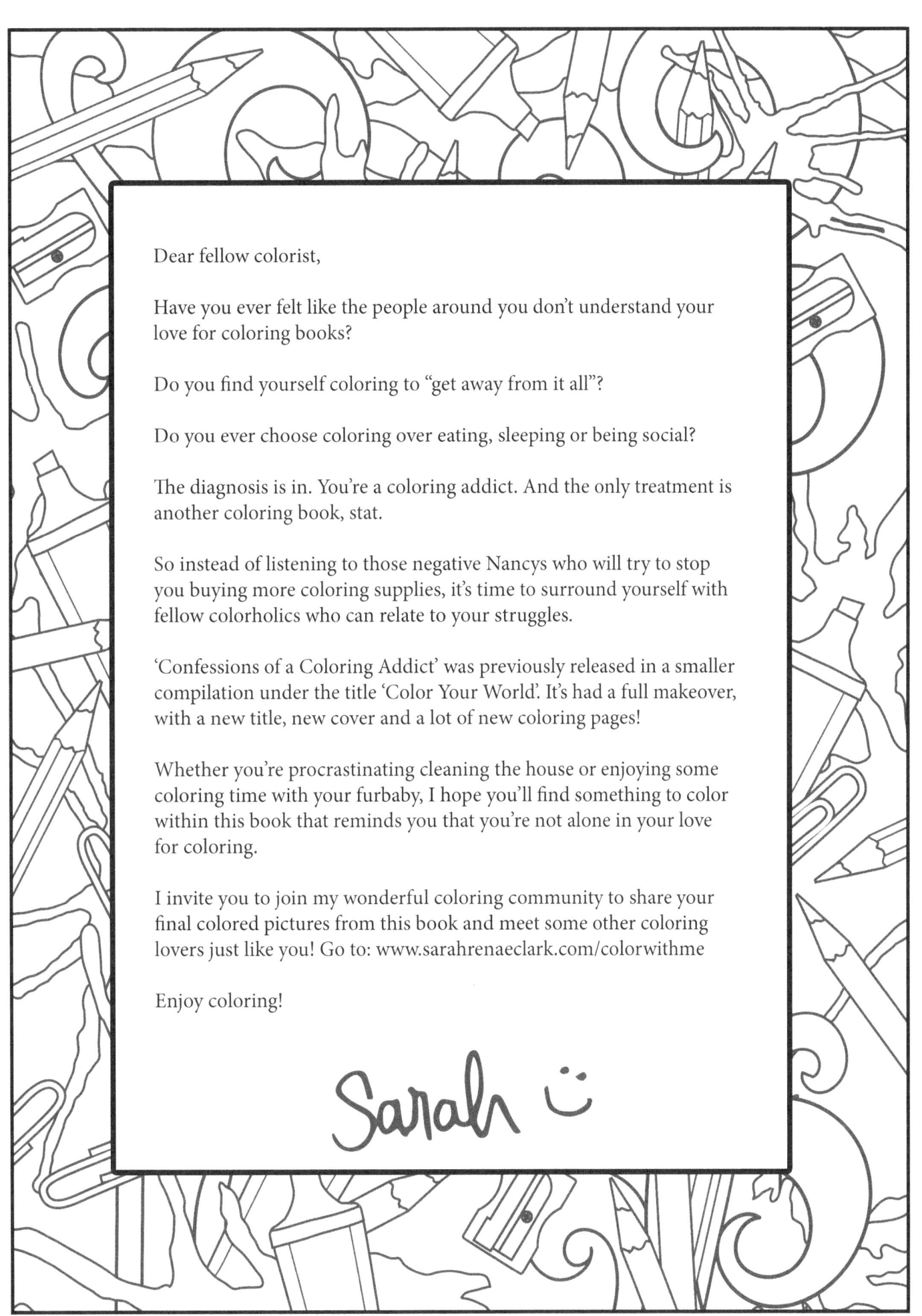

Dear fellow colorist,

Have you ever felt like the people around you don't understand your love for coloring books?

Do you find yourself coloring to "get away from it all"?

Do you ever choose coloring over eating, sleeping or being social?

The diagnosis is in. You're a coloring addict. And the only treatment is another coloring book, stat.

So instead of listening to those negative Nancys who will try to stop you buying more coloring supplies, it's time to surround yourself with fellow colorholics who can relate to your struggles.

'Confessions of a Coloring Addict' was previously released in a smaller compilation under the title 'Color Your World'. It's had a full makeover, with a new title, new cover and a lot of new coloring pages!

Whether you're procrastinating cleaning the house or enjoying some coloring time with your furbaby, I hope you'll find something to color within this book that reminds you that you're not alone in your love for coloring.

I invite you to join my wonderful coloring community to share your final colored pictures from this book and meet some other coloring lovers just like you! Go to: www.sarahrenaeclark.com/colorwithme

Enjoy coloring!

Sarah :)

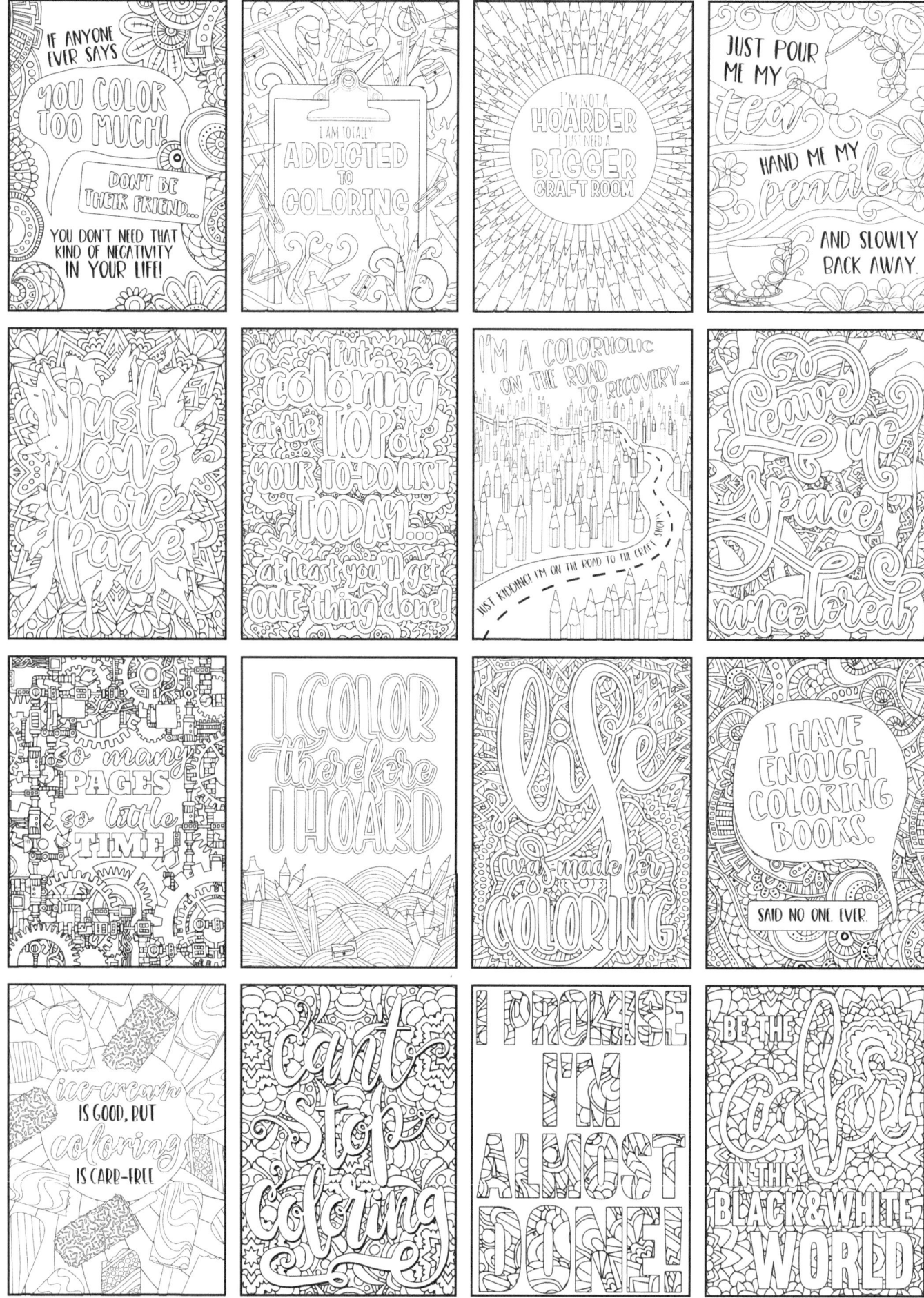

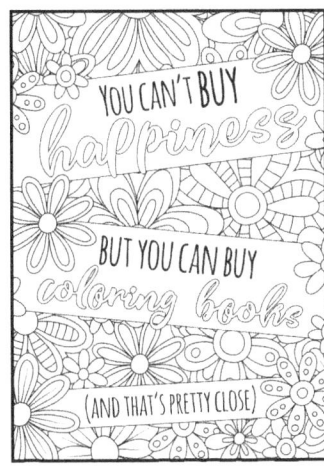

YOU CAN'T BUY *happiness* BUT YOU CAN BUY *coloring books* (AND THAT'S PRETTY CLOSE)

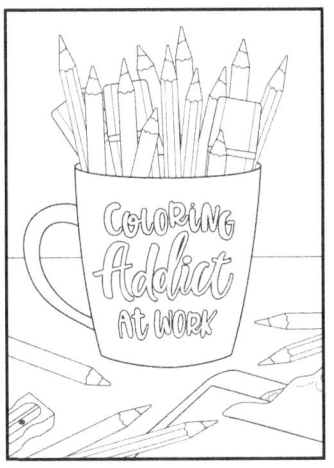

Coloring Addict AT WORK

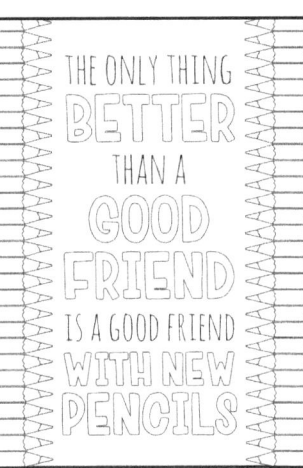

THE ONLY THING BETTER THAN A GOOD FRIEND IS A GOOD FRIEND WITH NEW PENCILS

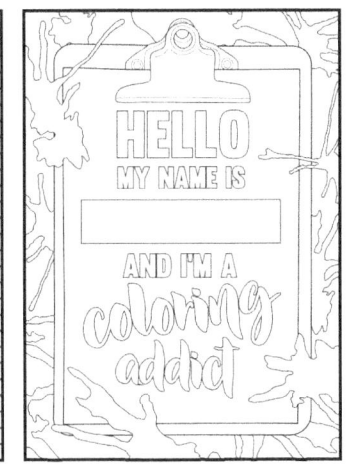

HELLO MY NAME IS AND I'M A *coloring addict*

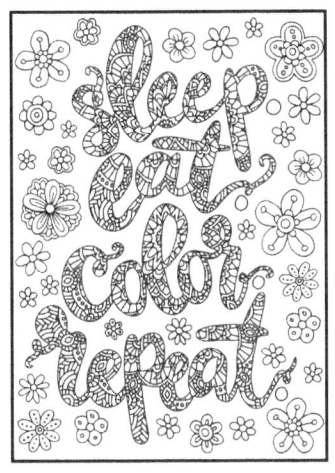

sleep eat color repeat

SHARE YOUR ADDICTION

Share your beautiful colored pages from this book on social media

@sarahrenaeclark

or upload them to my Facebook group and see what everyone else is coloring!

www.sarahrenaeclark.com/colorwithme

COLOR *your stress away*

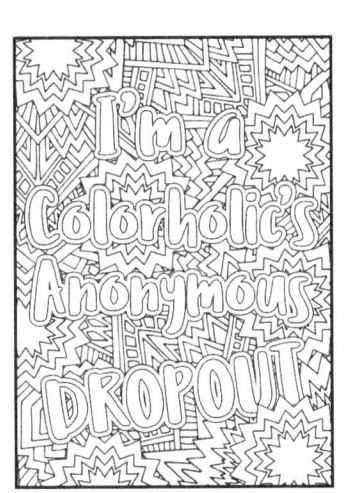

I'm a Colorholics Anonymous DROPOUT

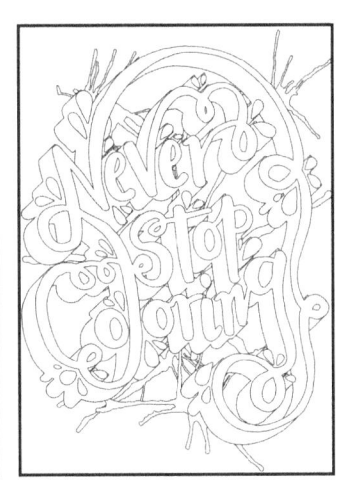

Never stop coloring

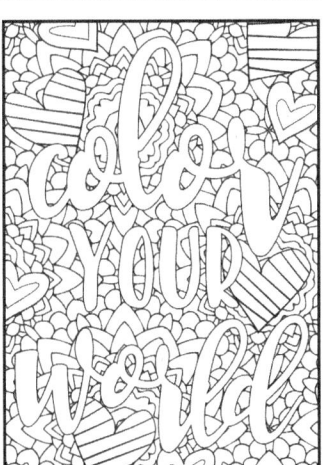

color your world

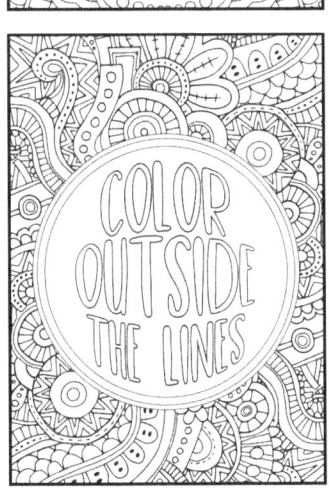

COLOR OUTSIDE THE LINES

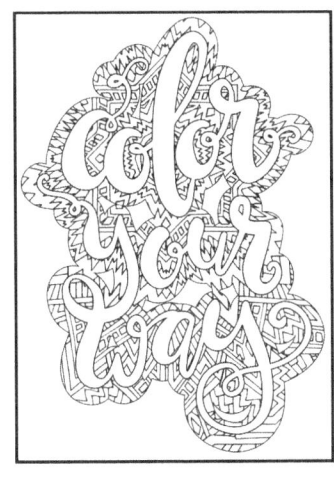

color your way

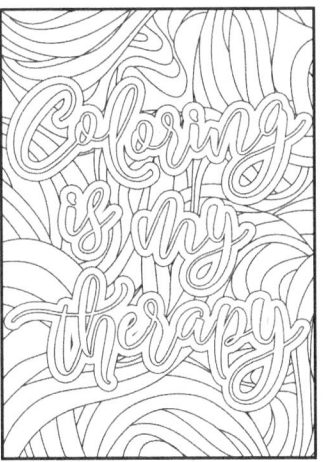

Coloring is my therapy

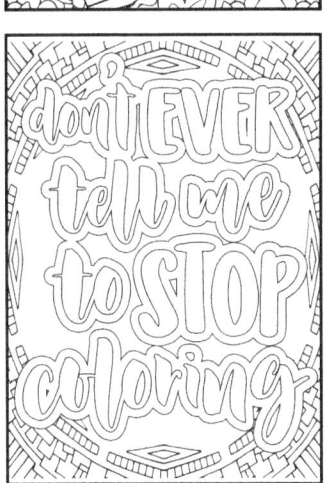

don't EVER tell me to STOP coloring

all the colors of the rainbow

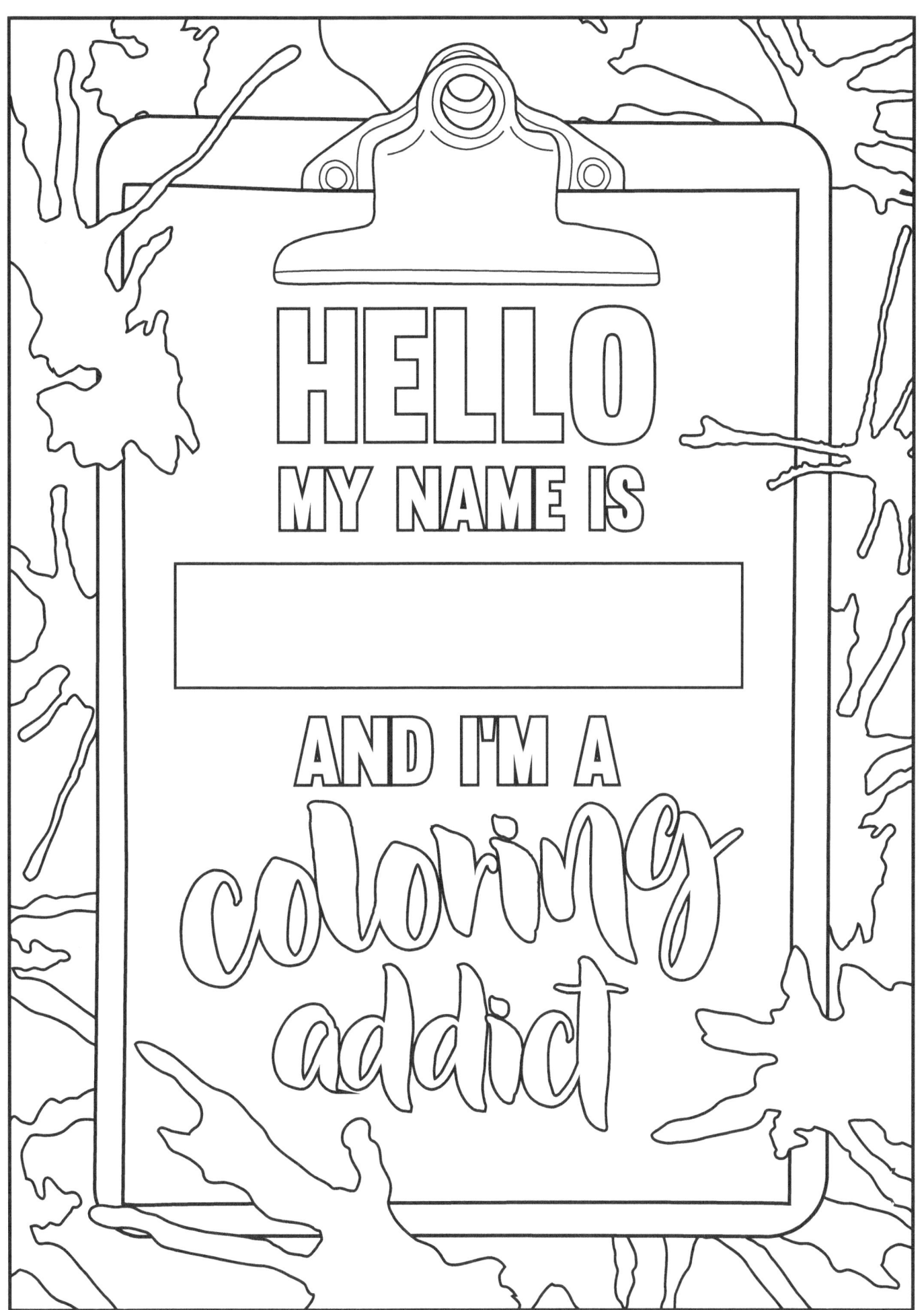

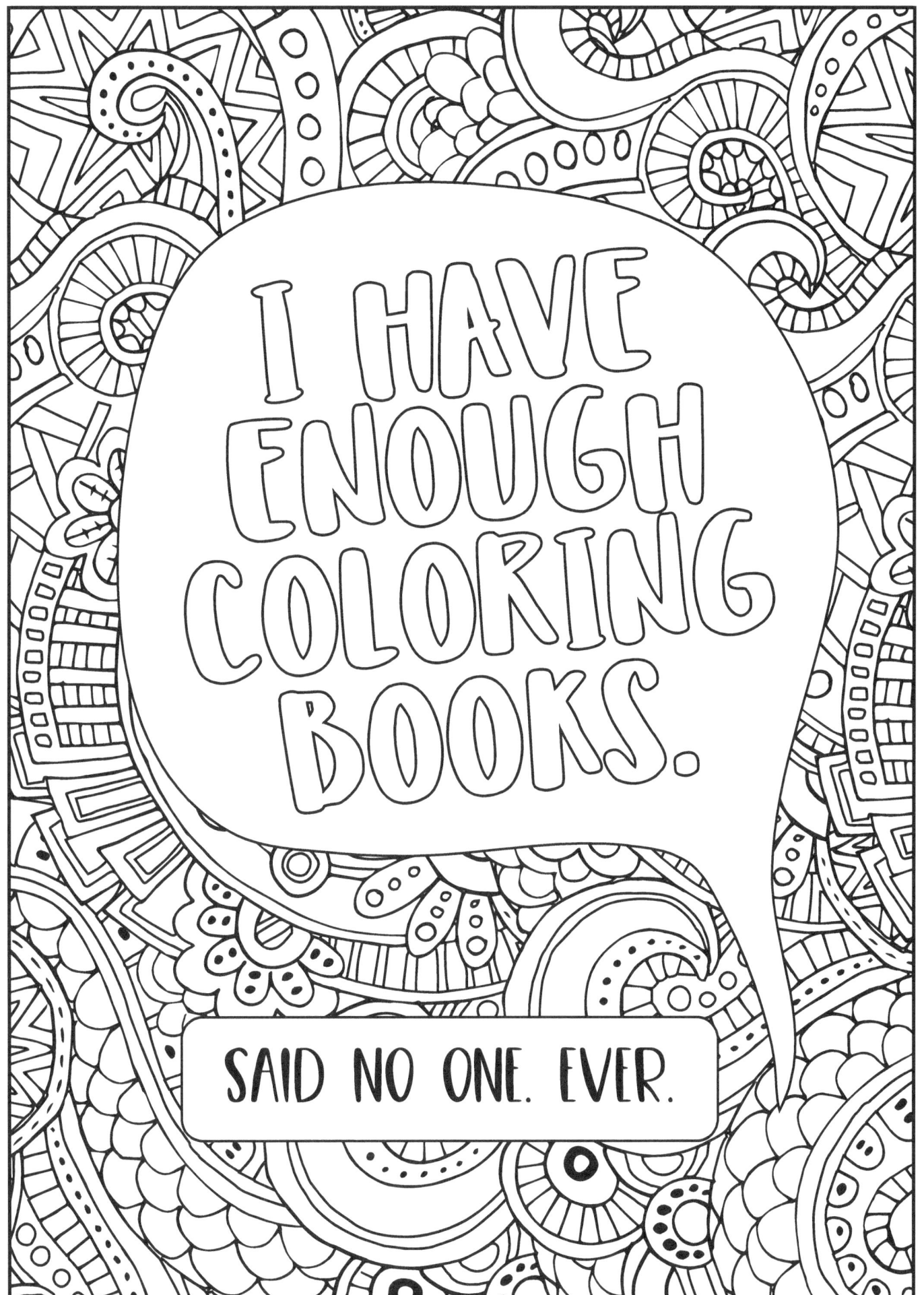

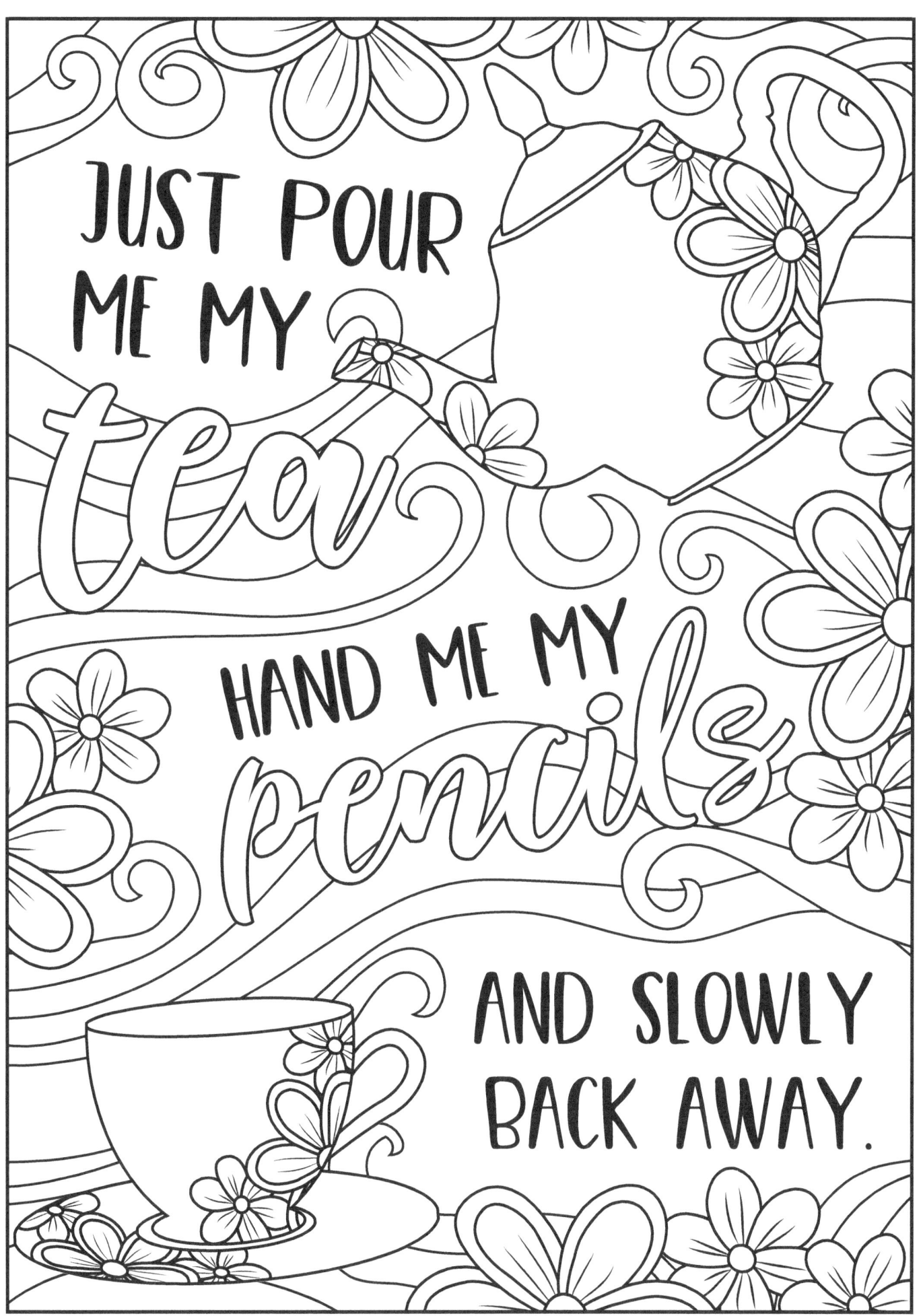

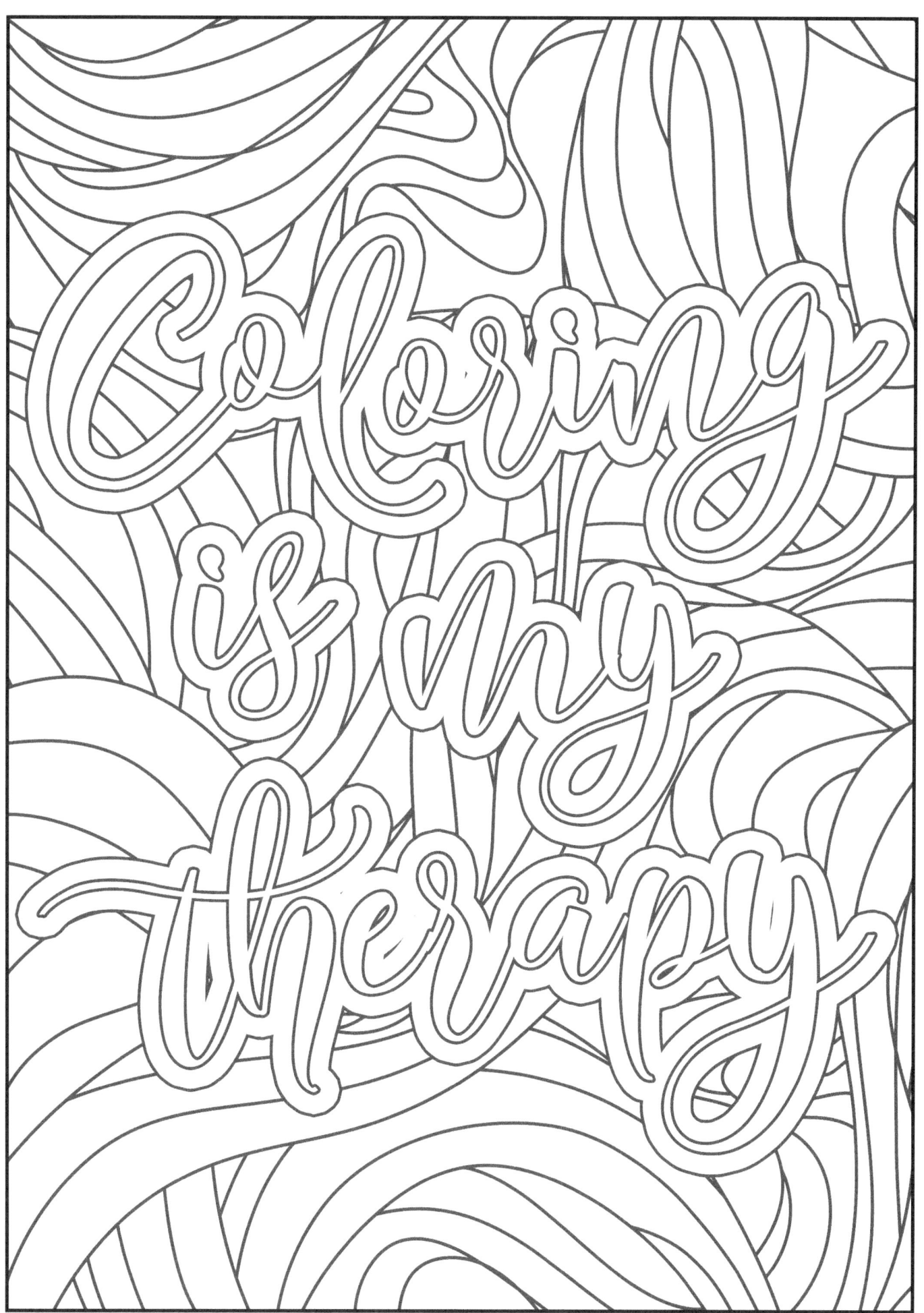

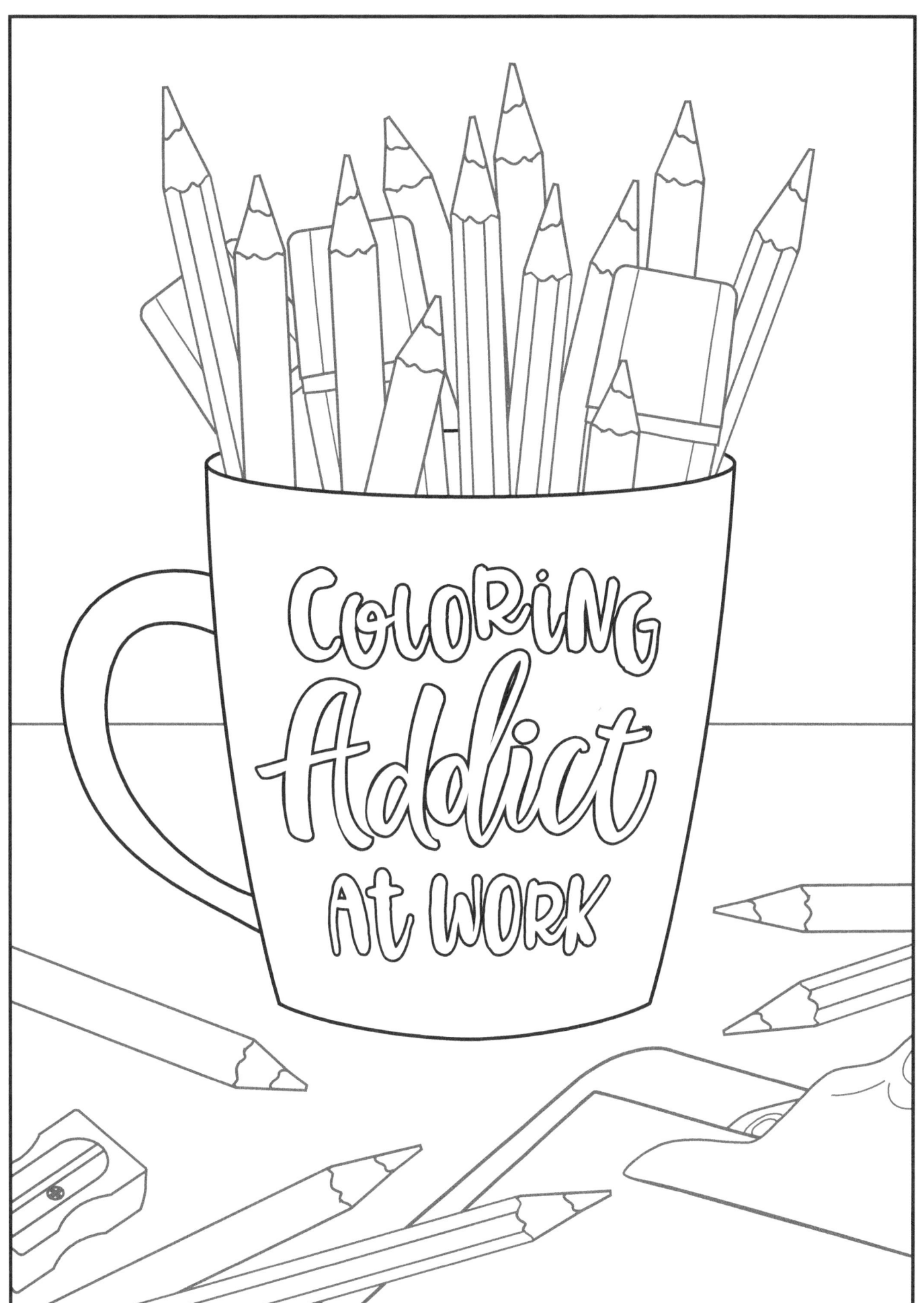

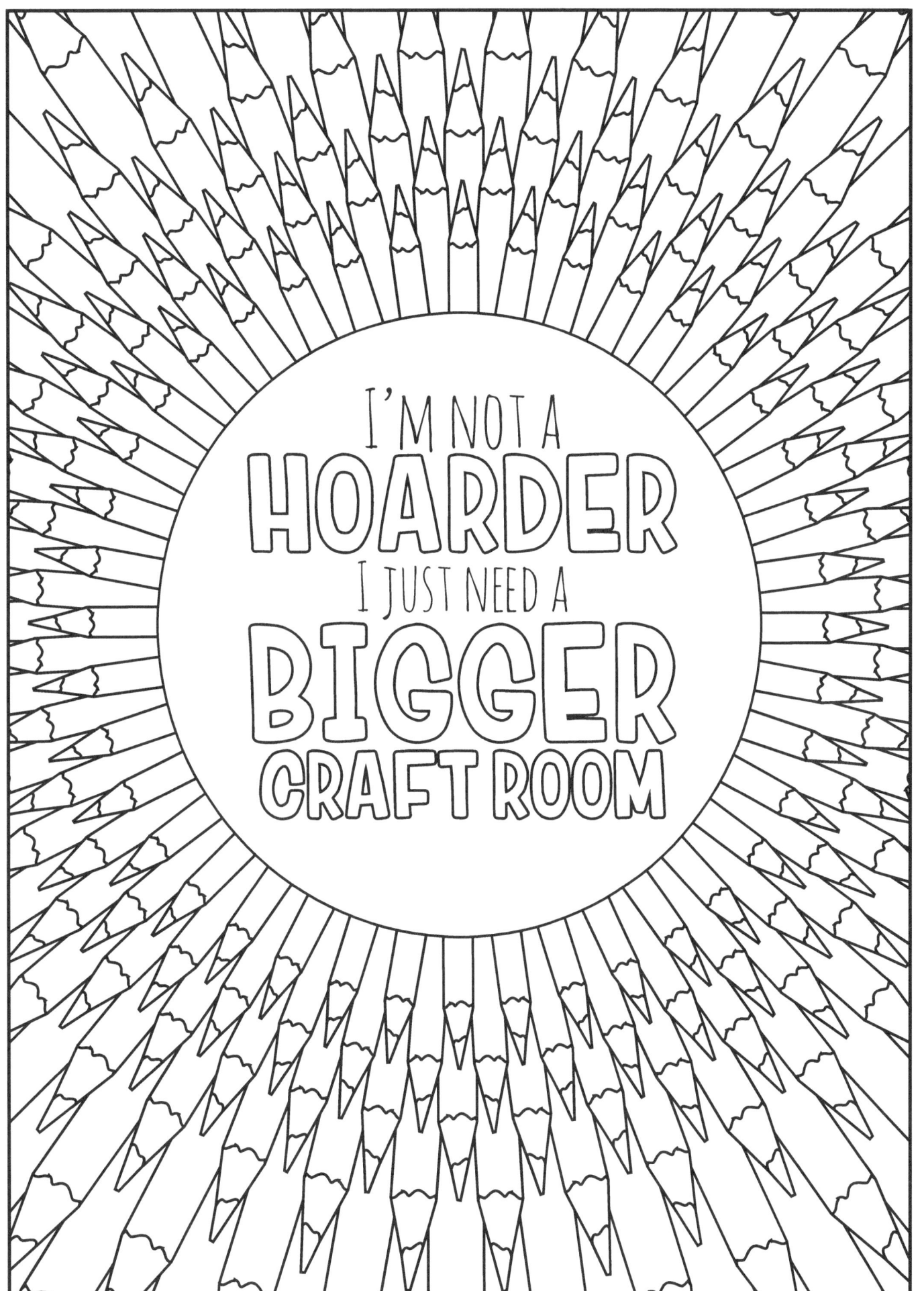

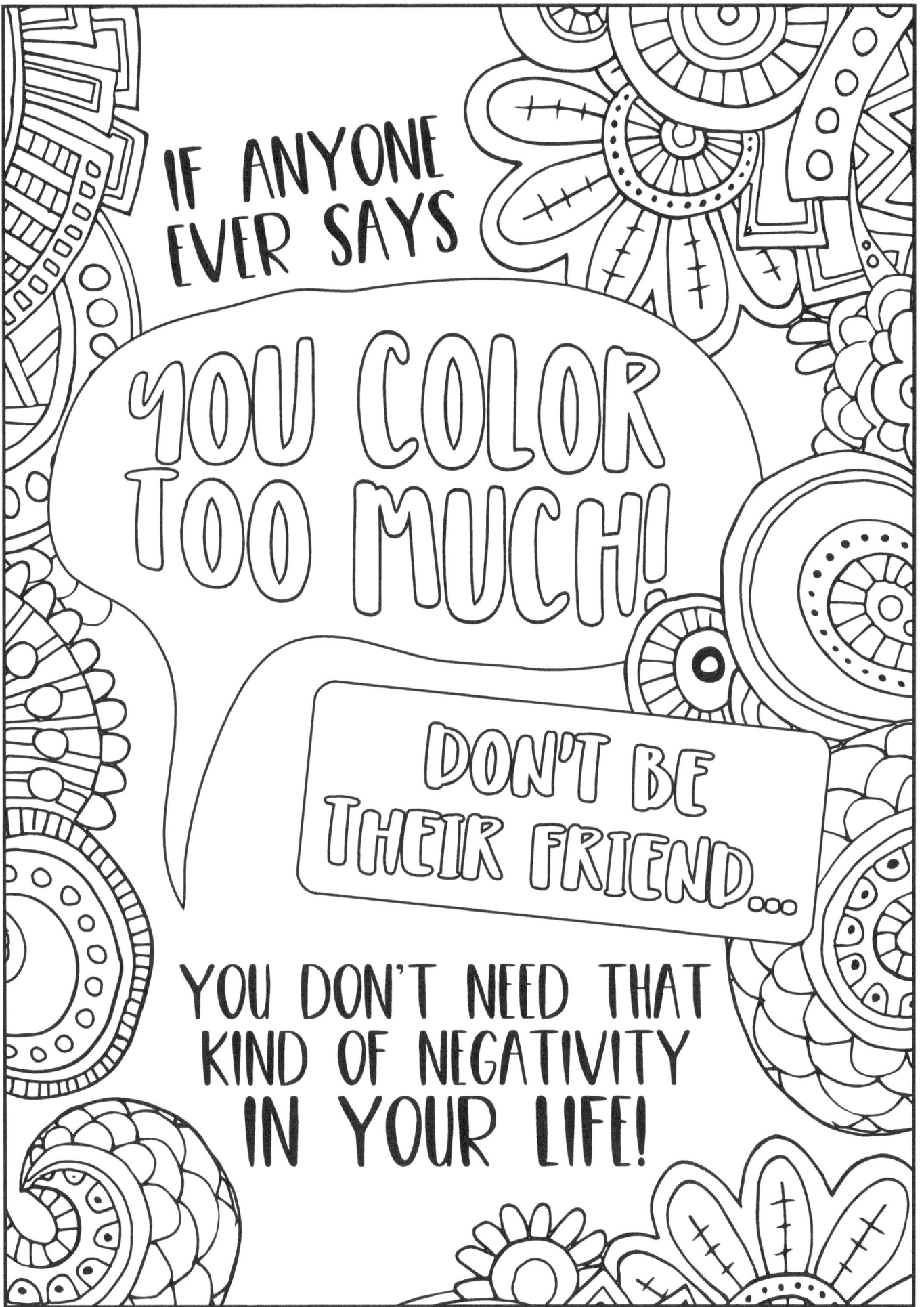

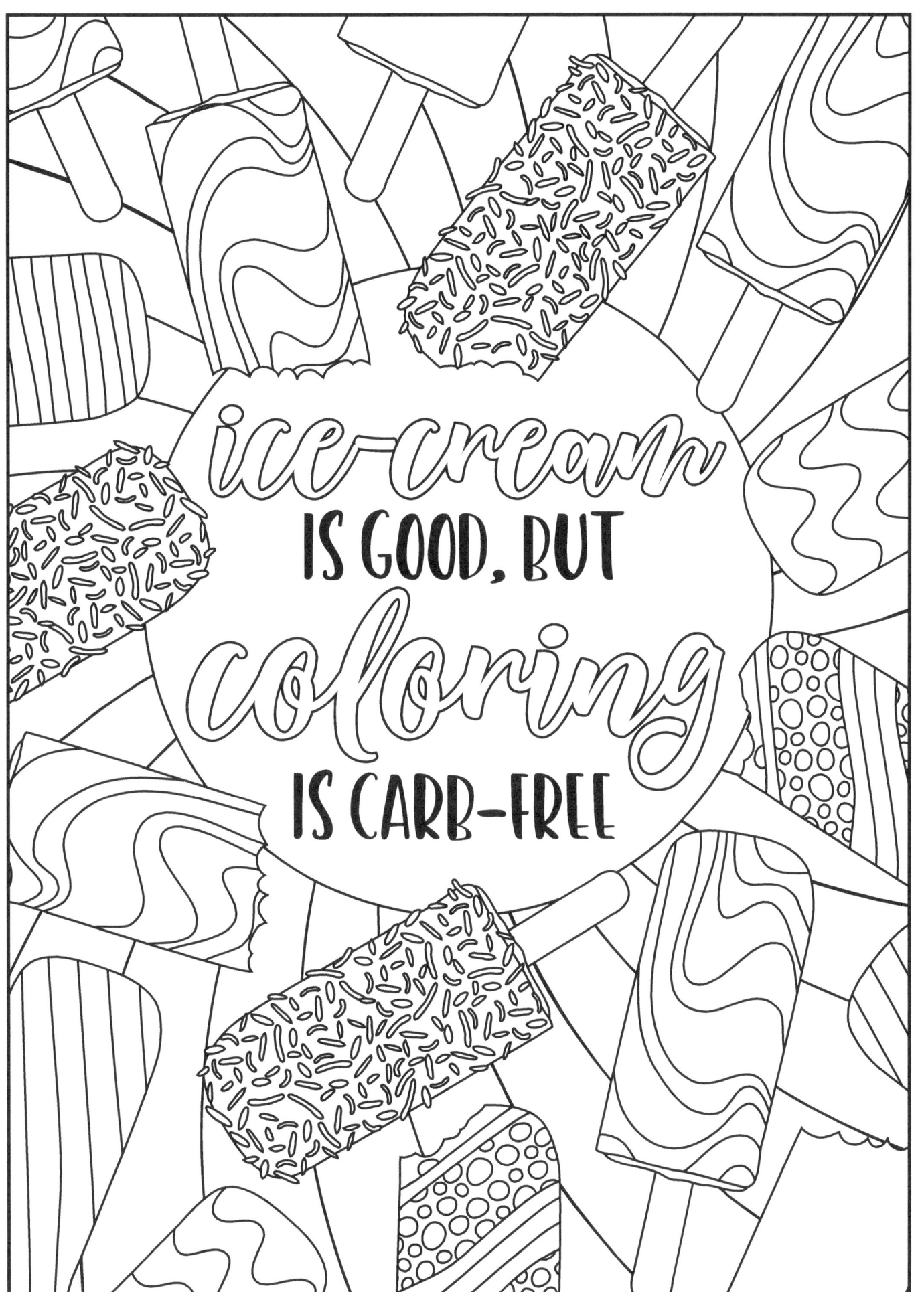

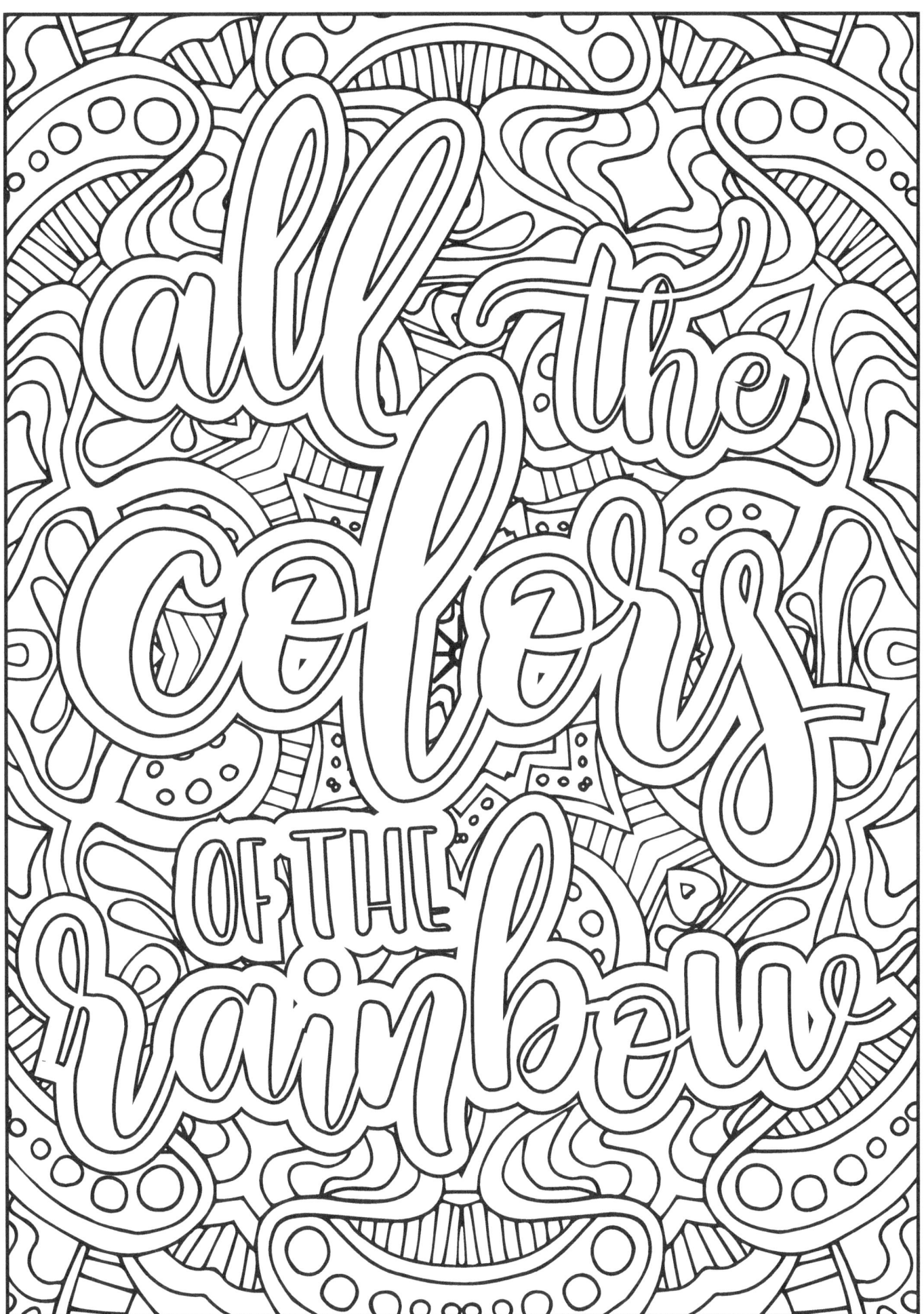

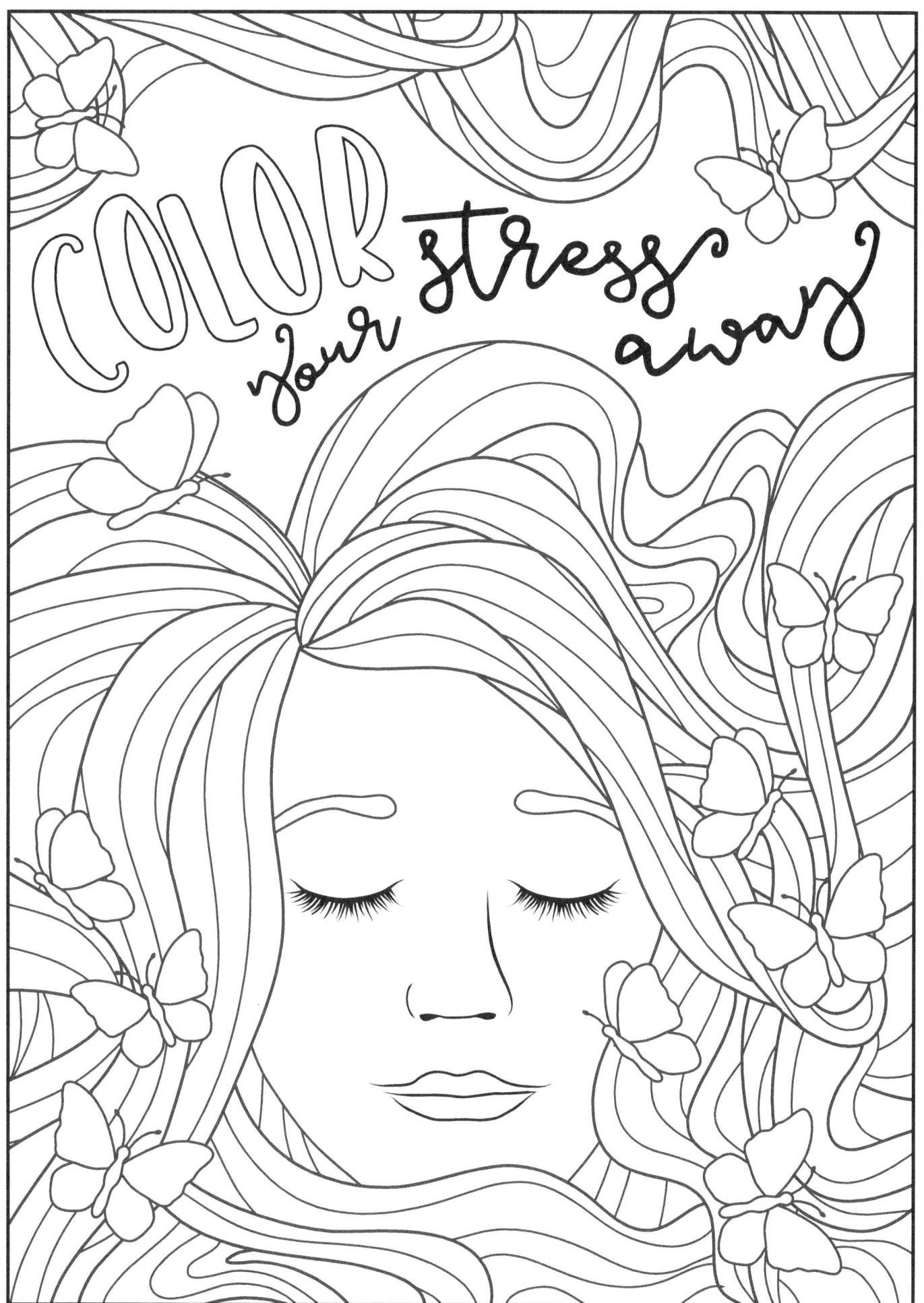

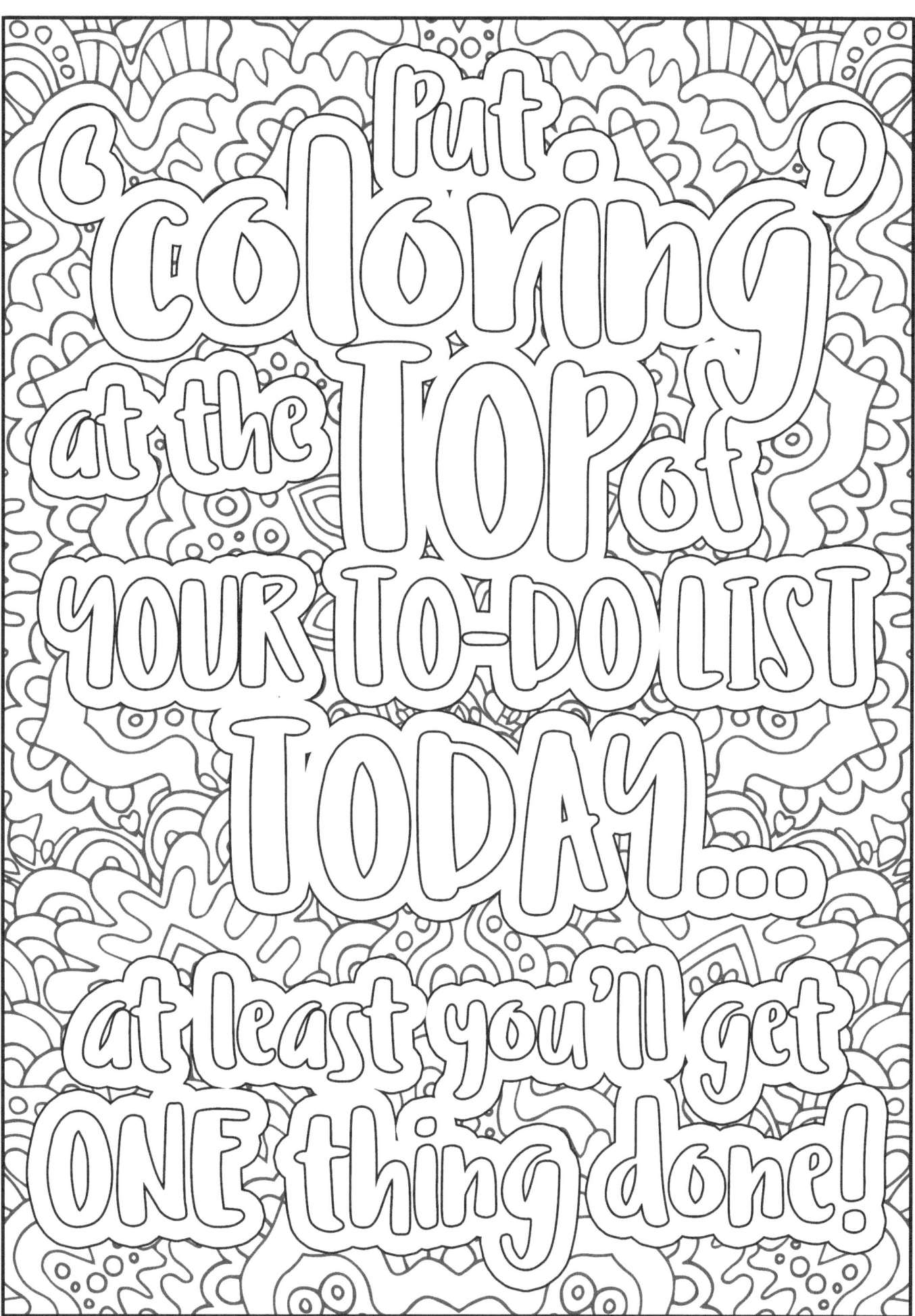

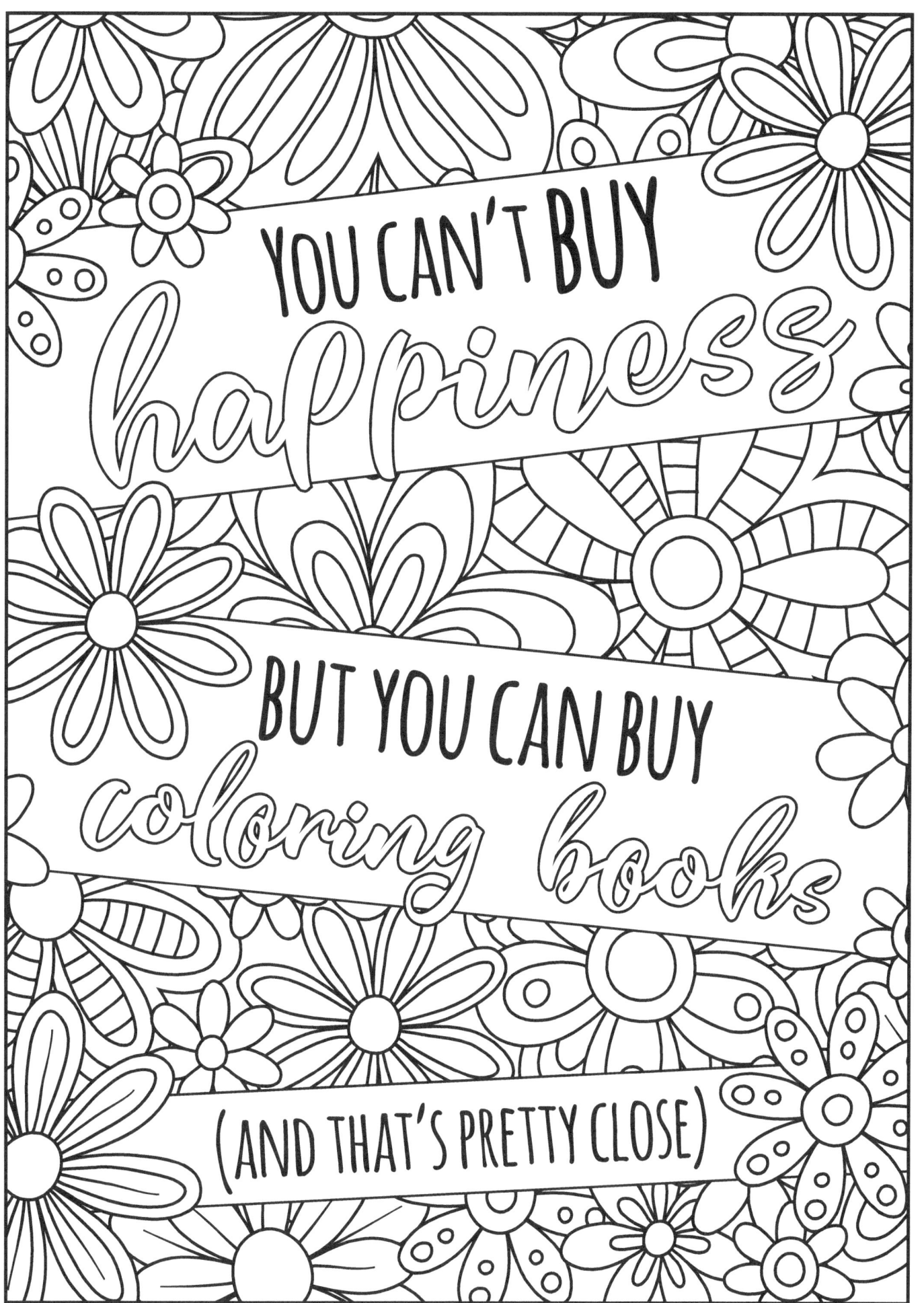

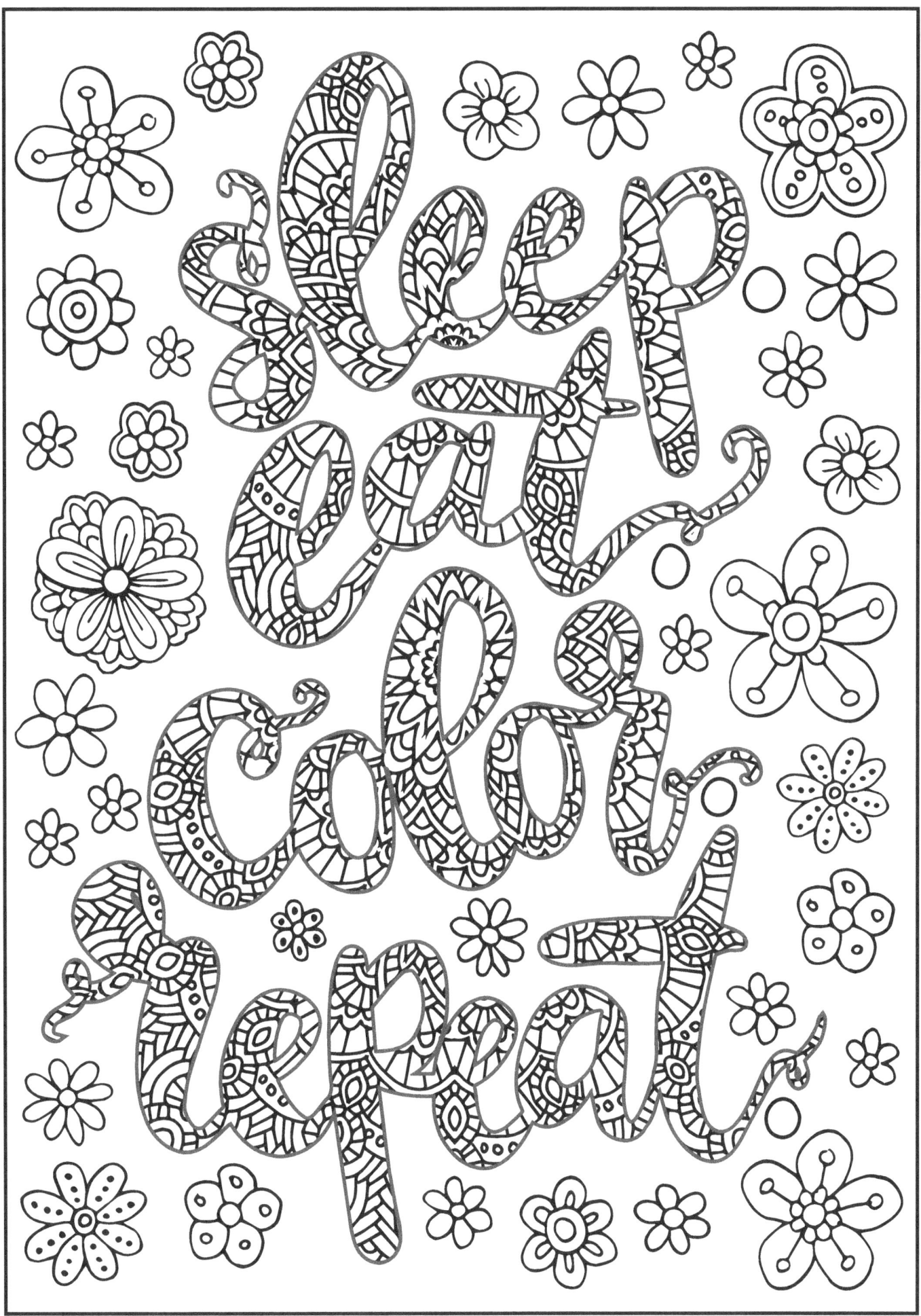

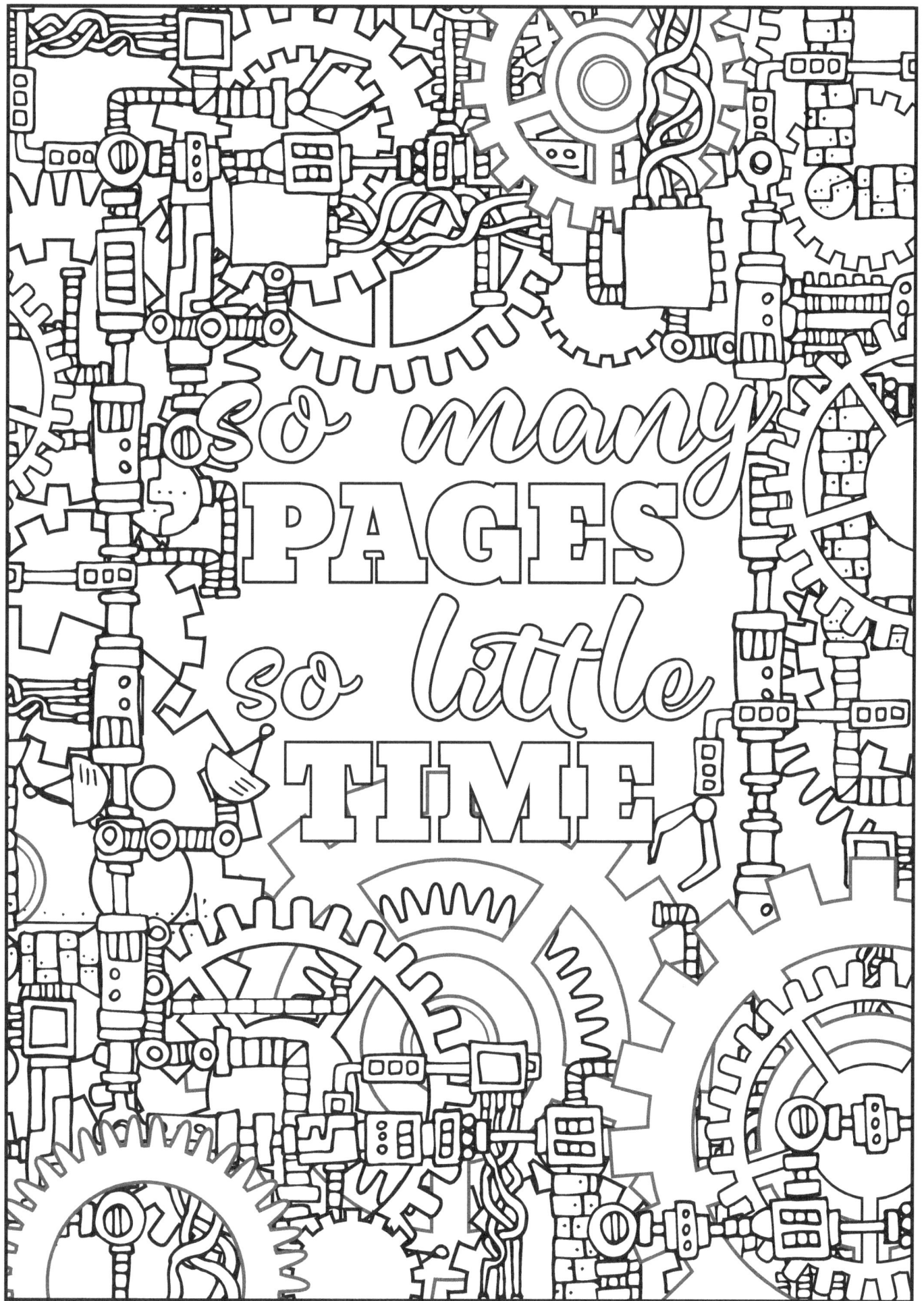

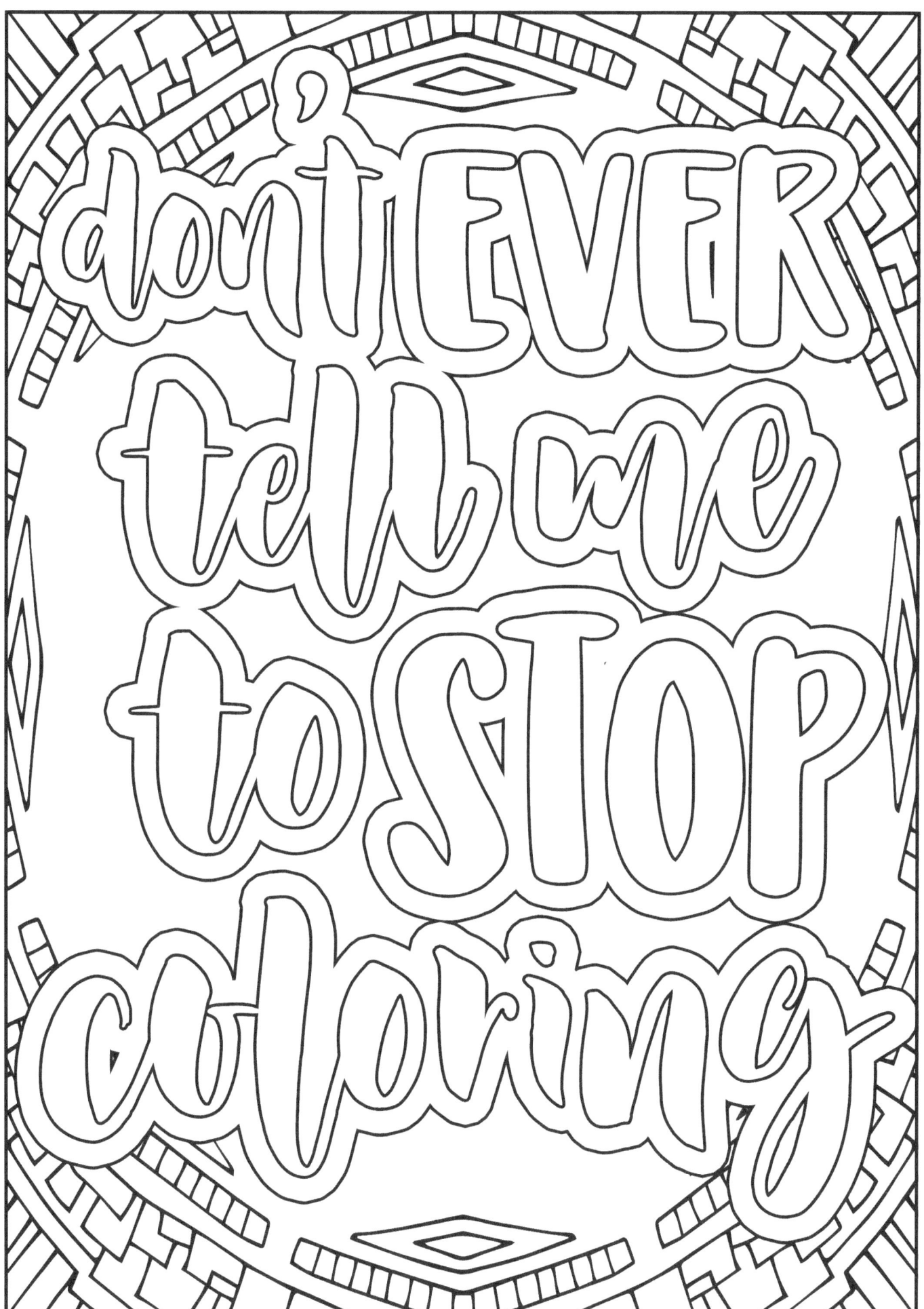

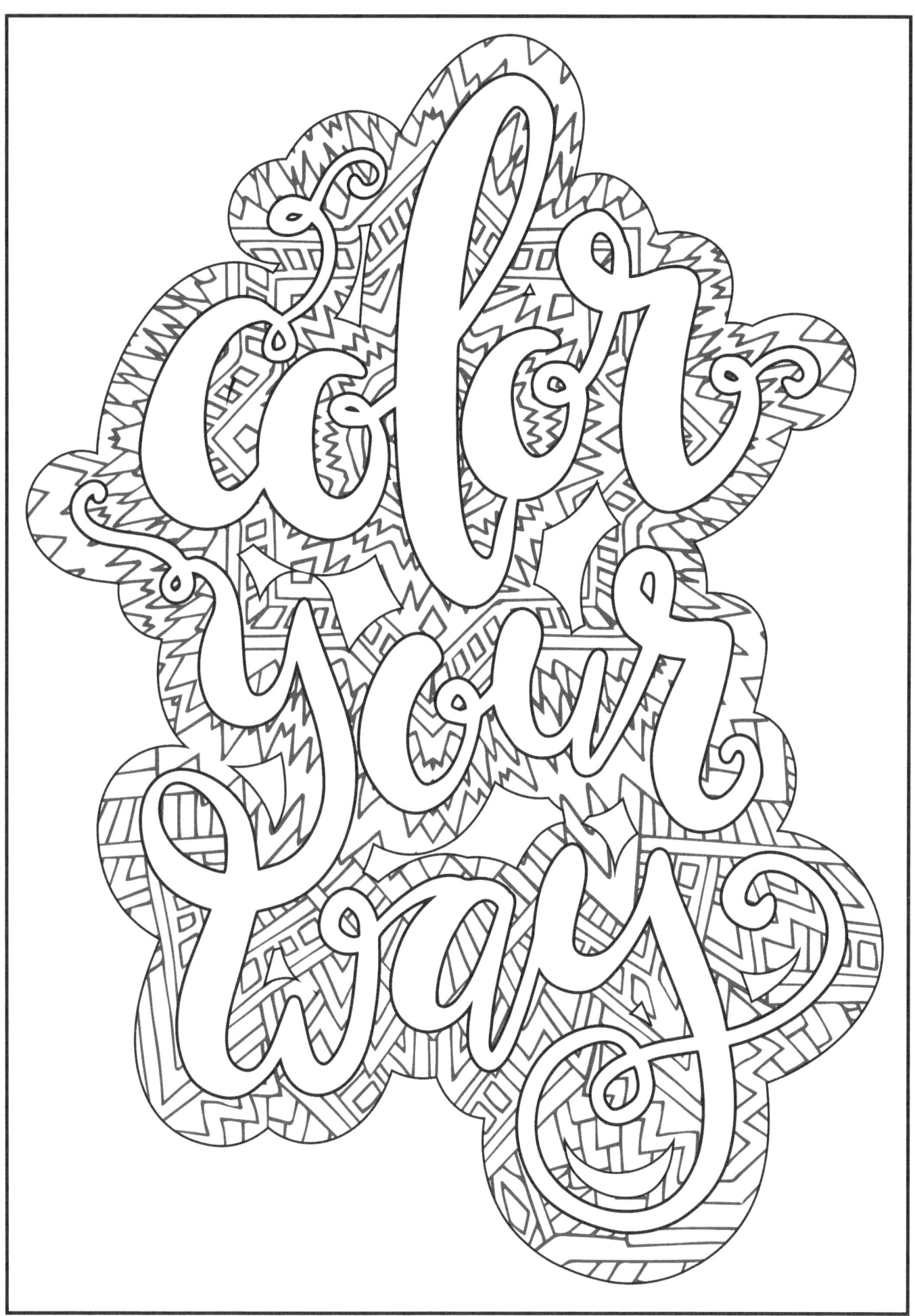

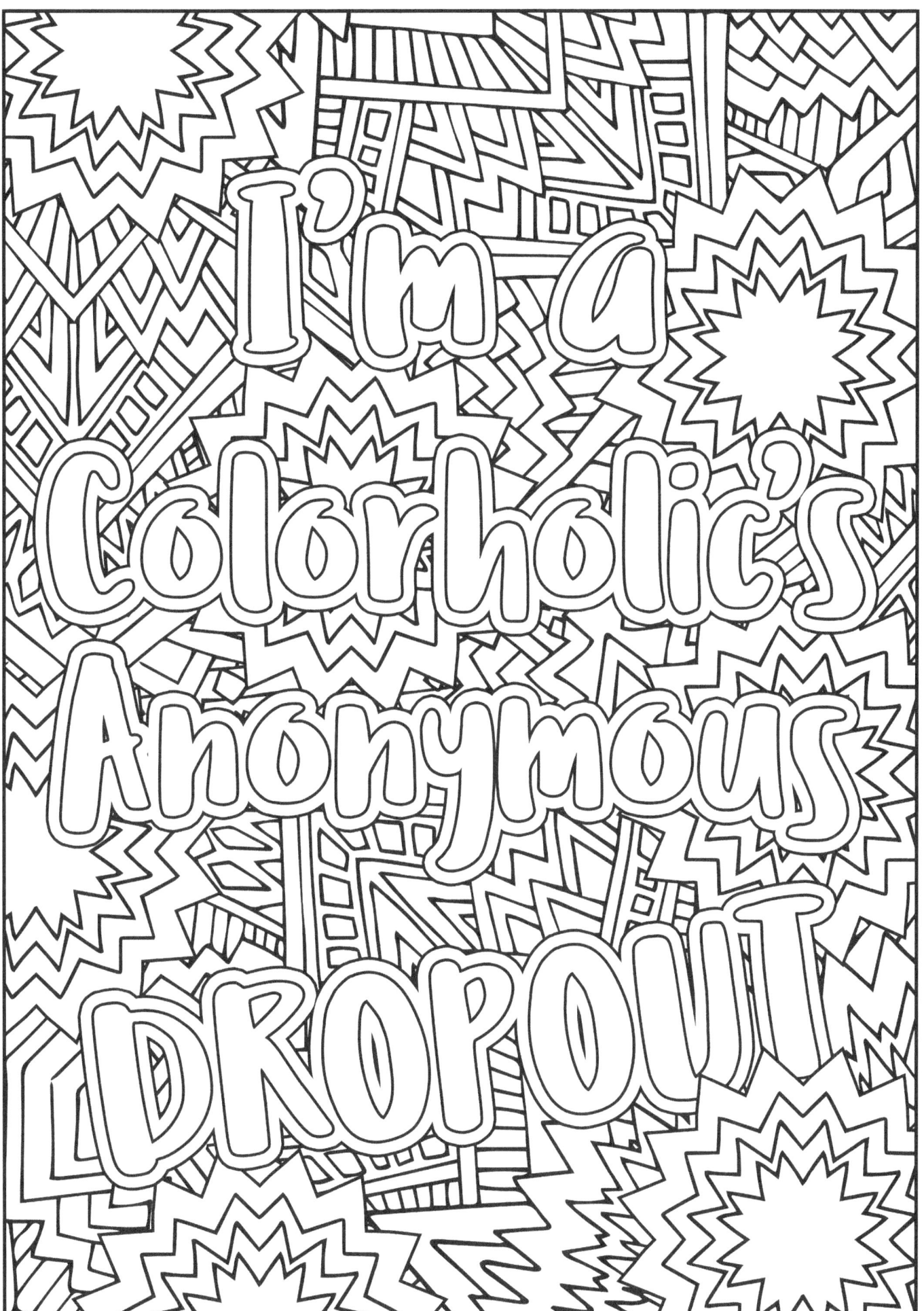

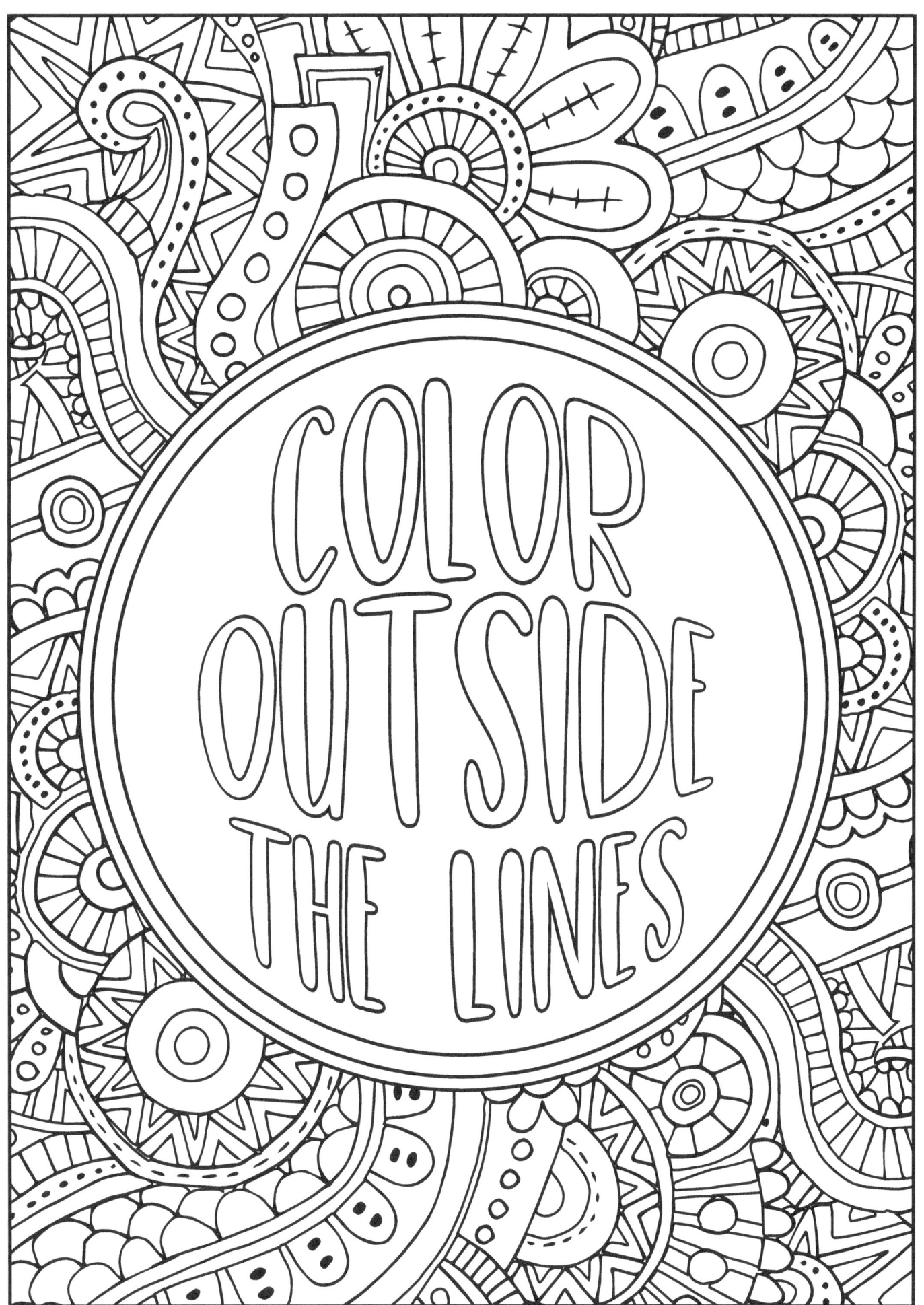

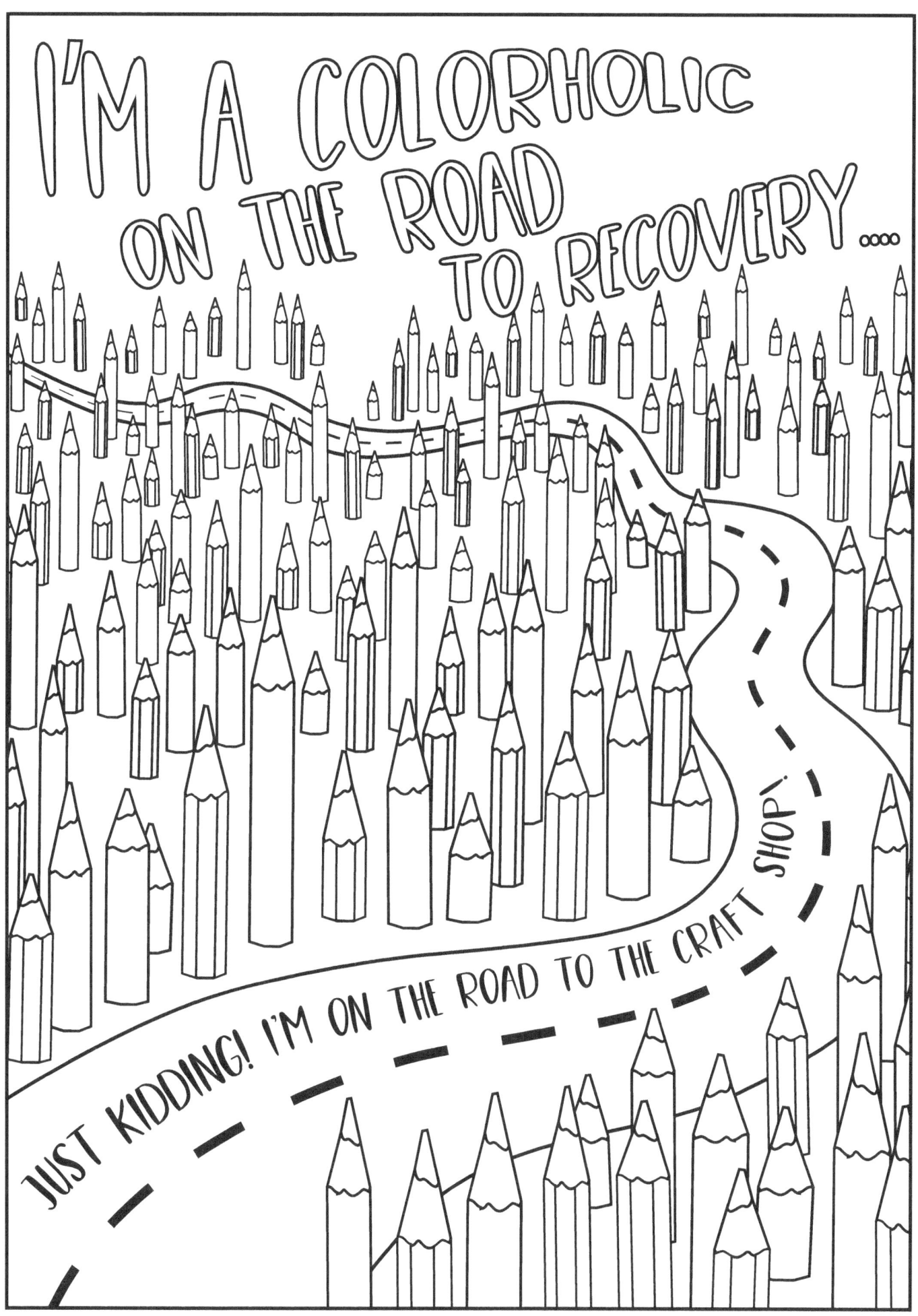

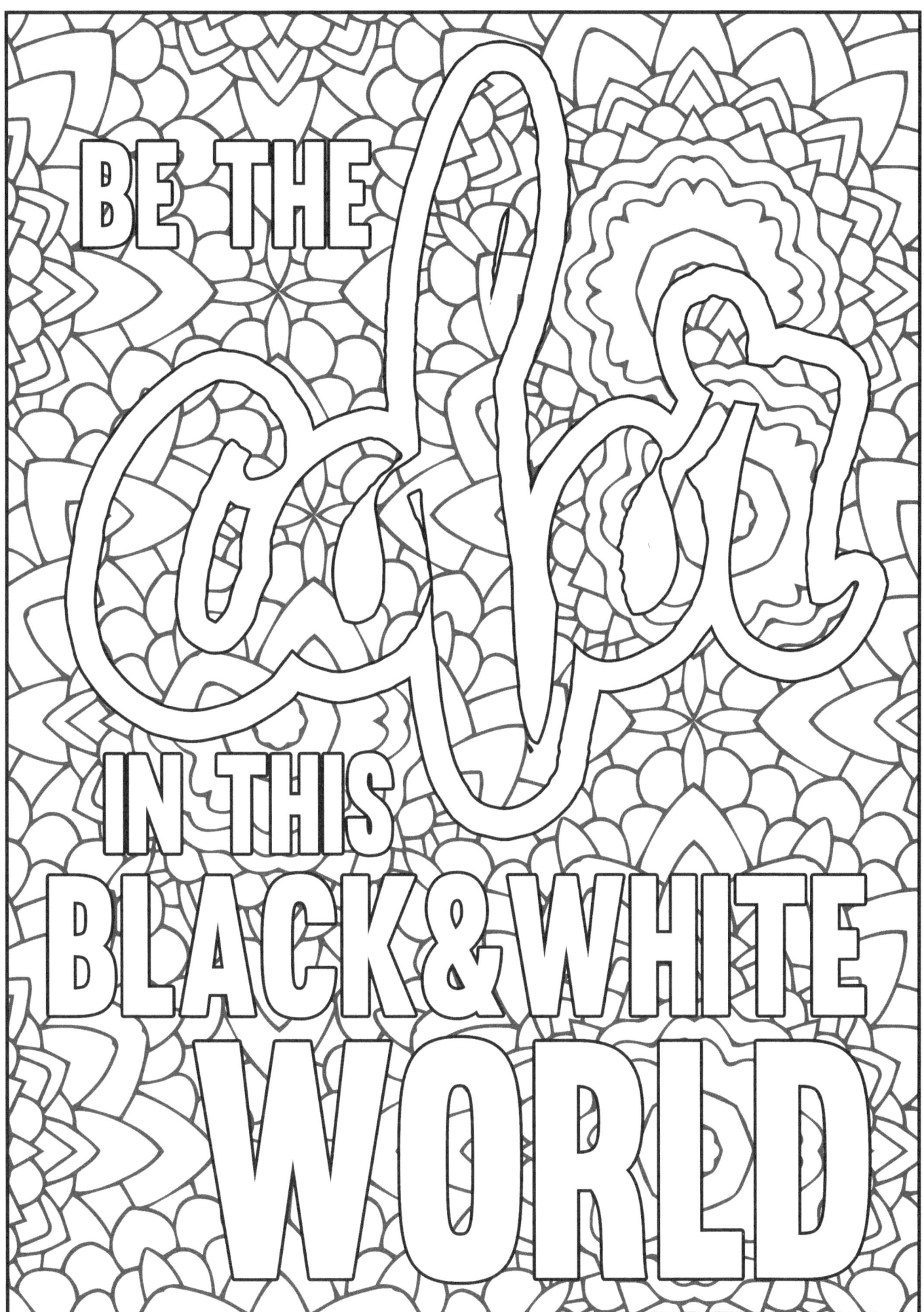

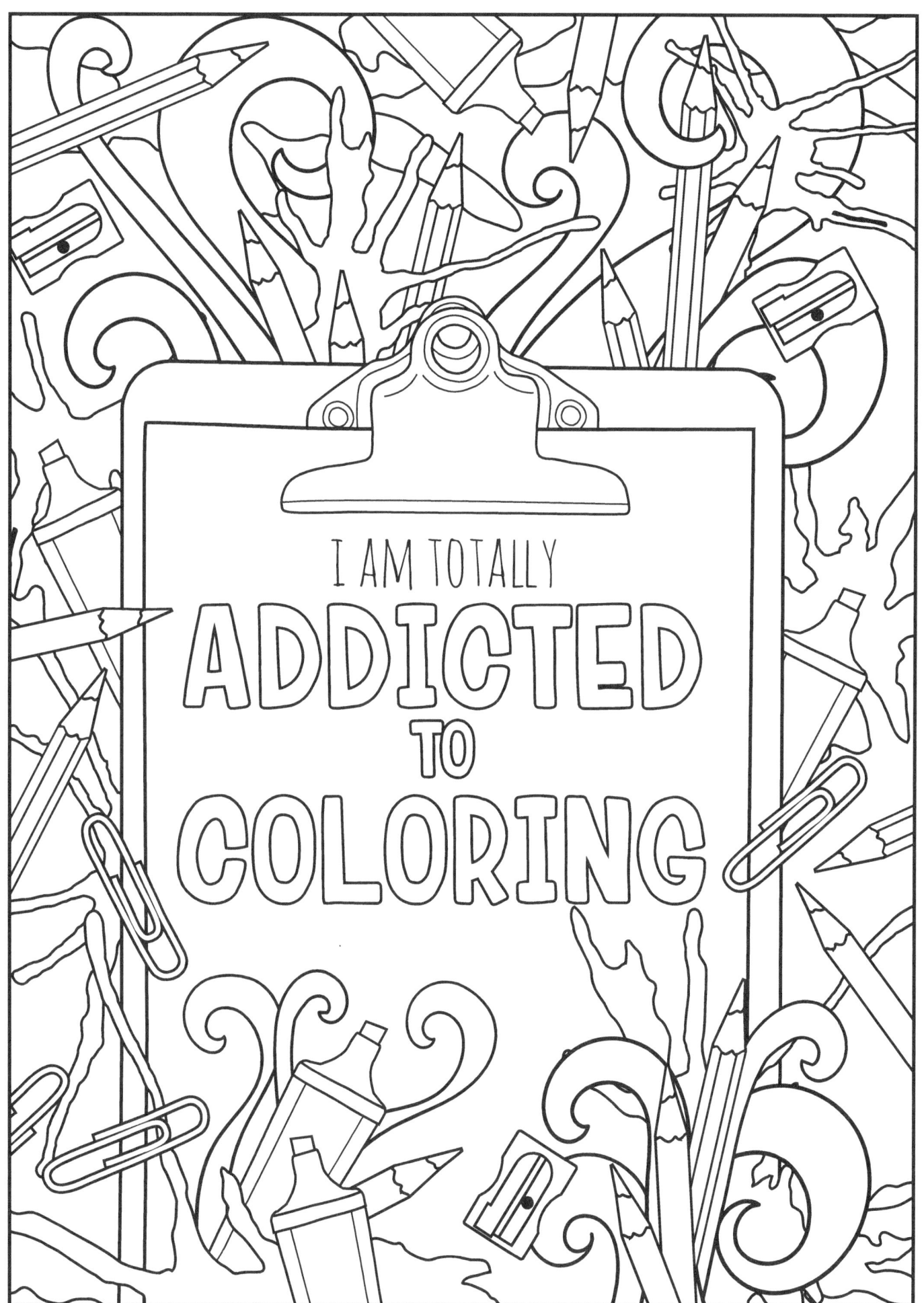

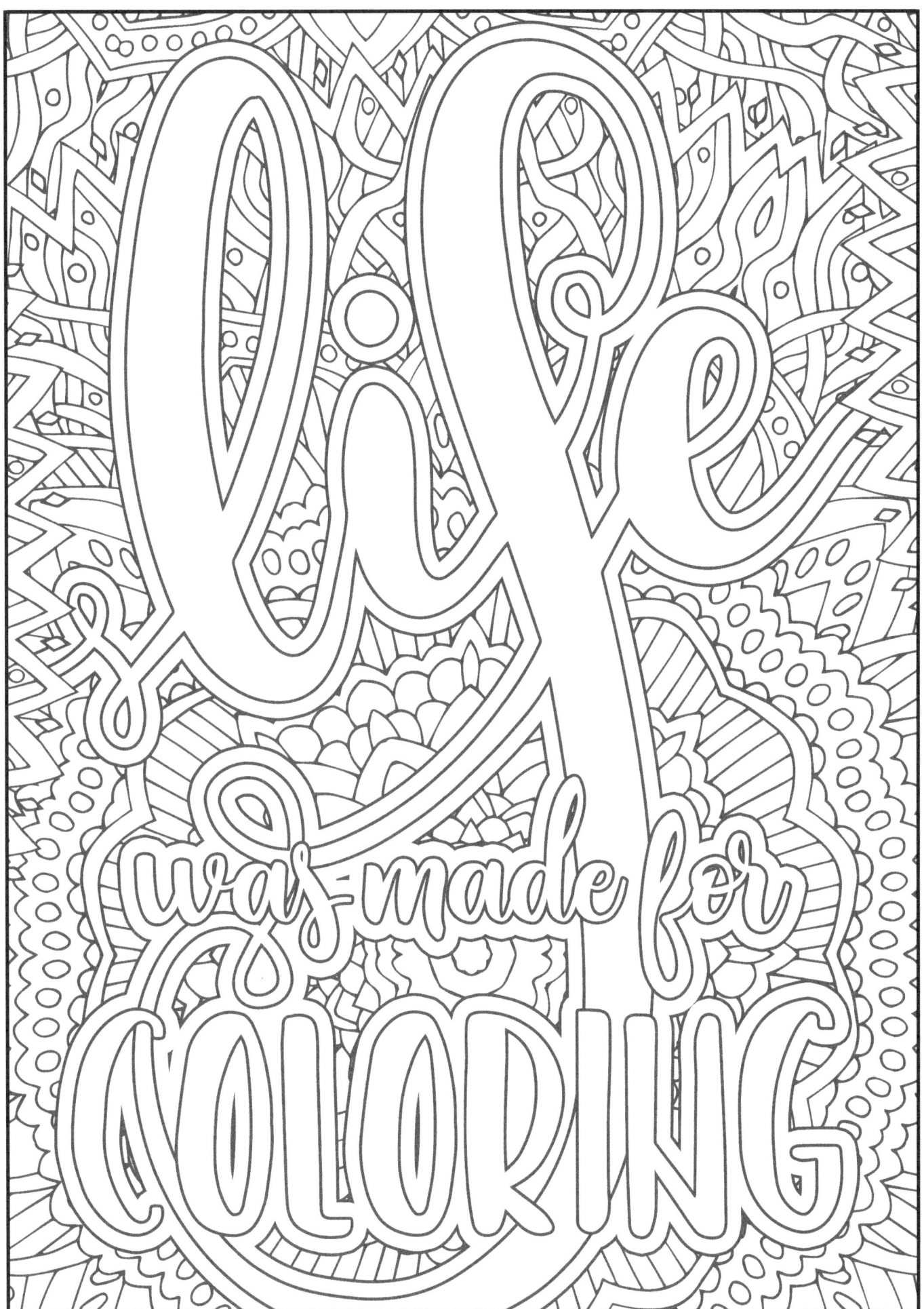

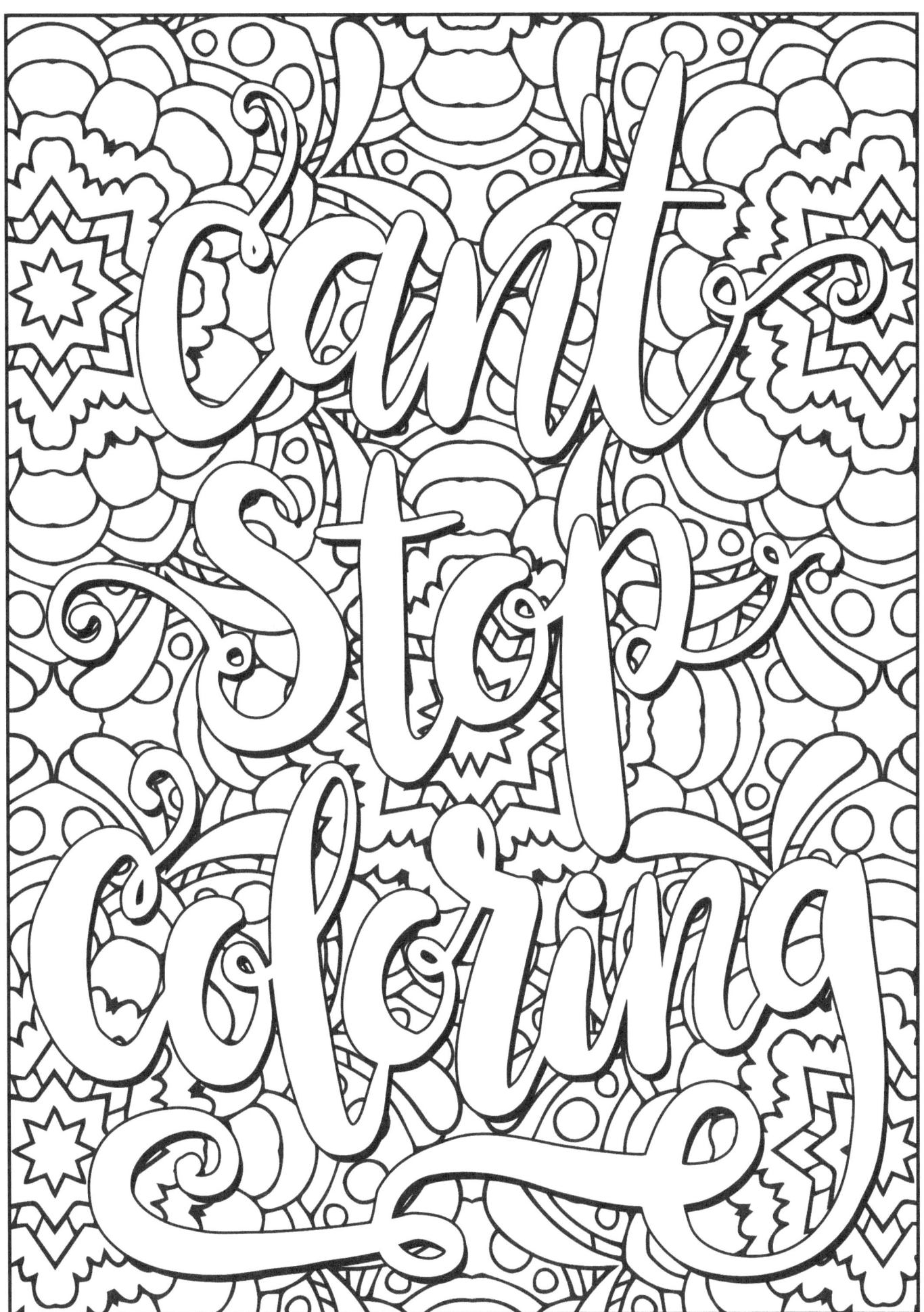

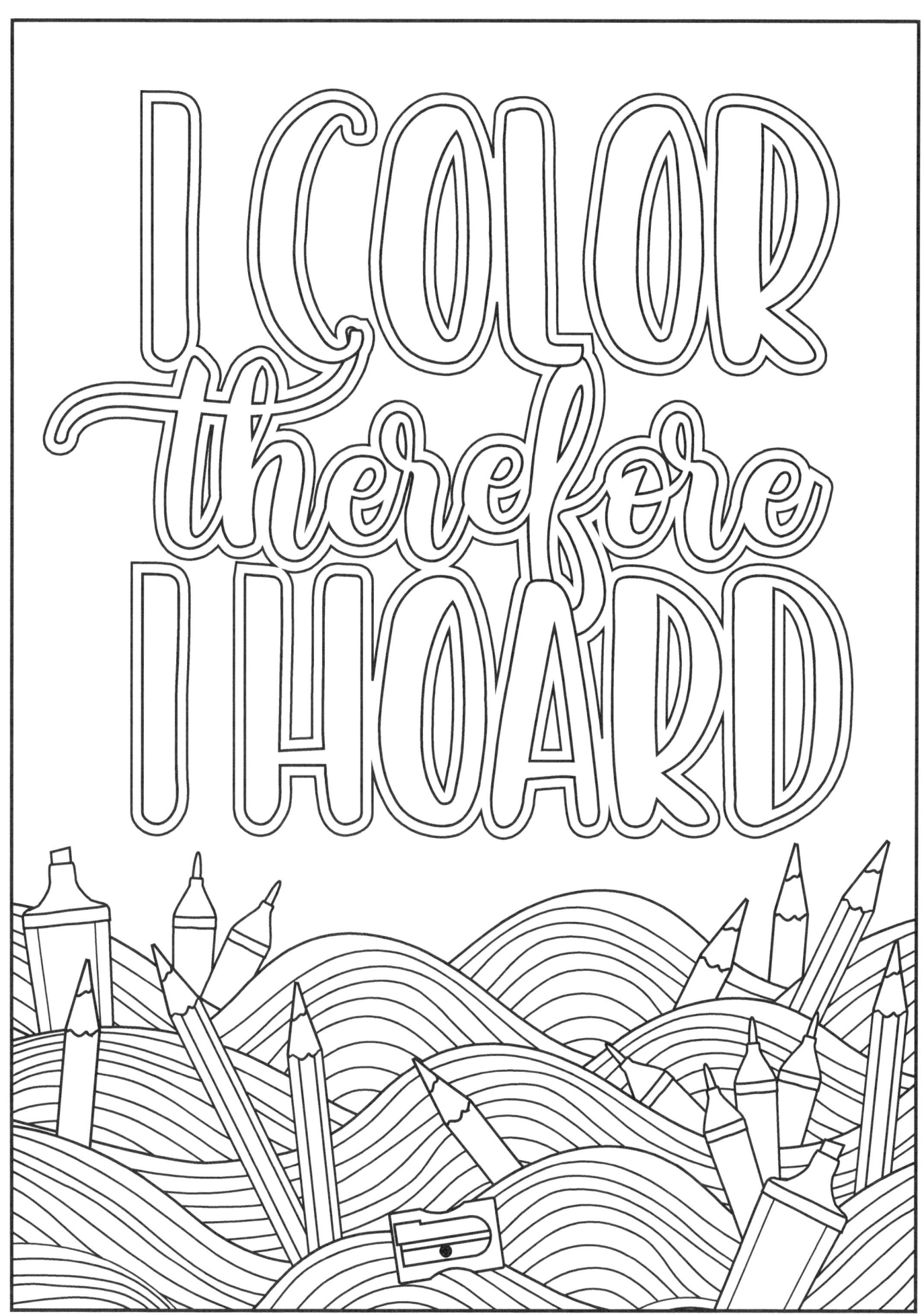

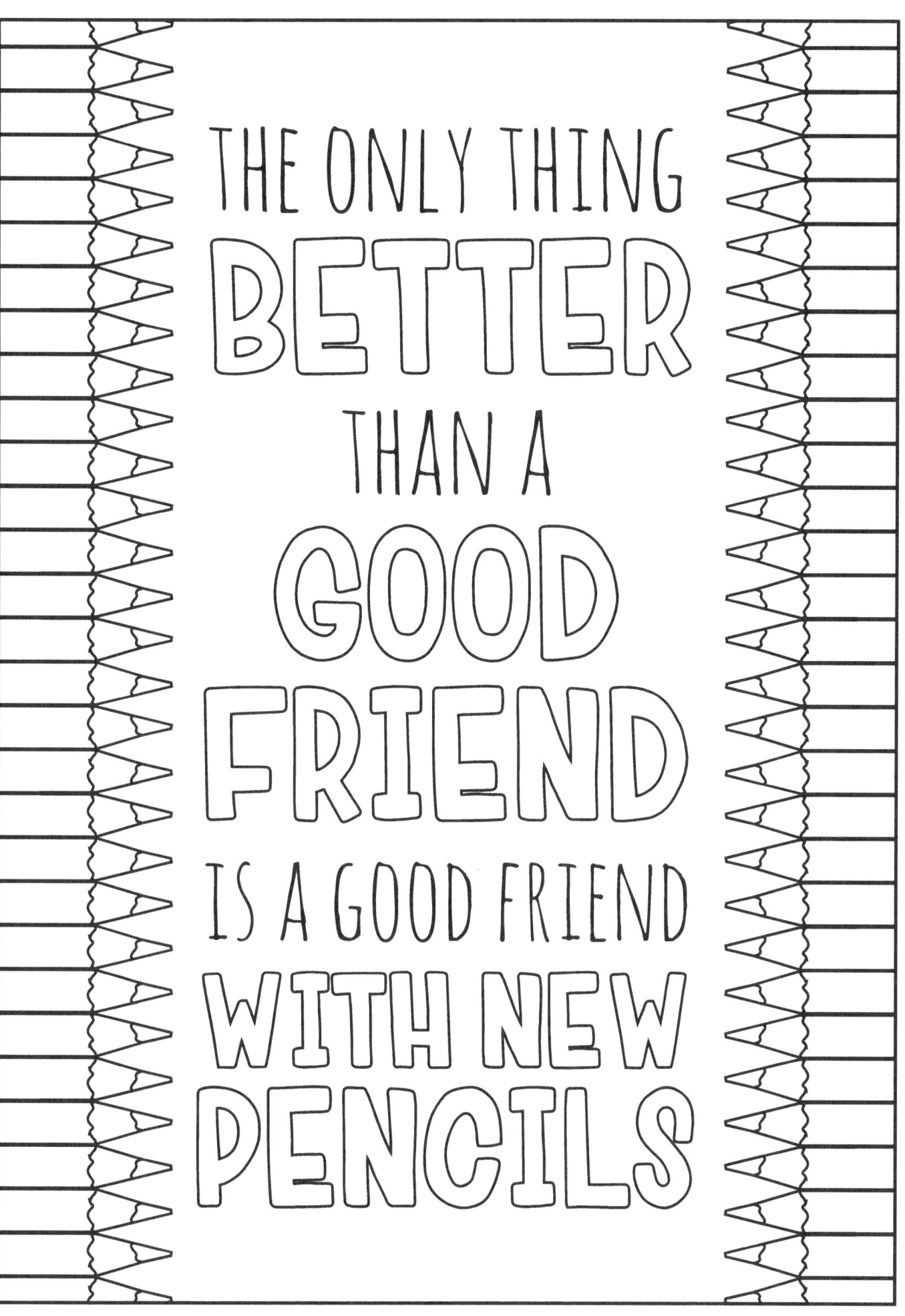

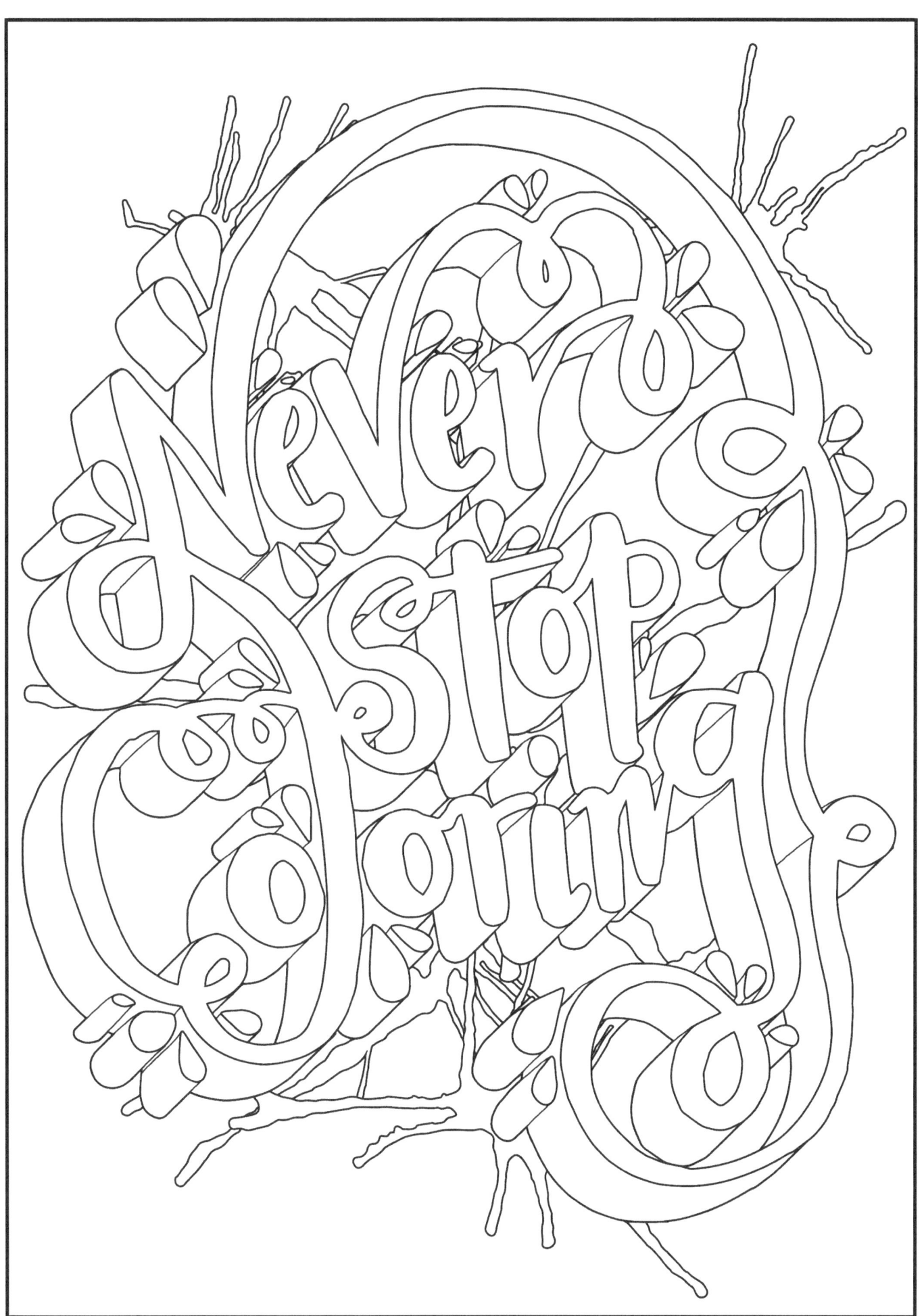

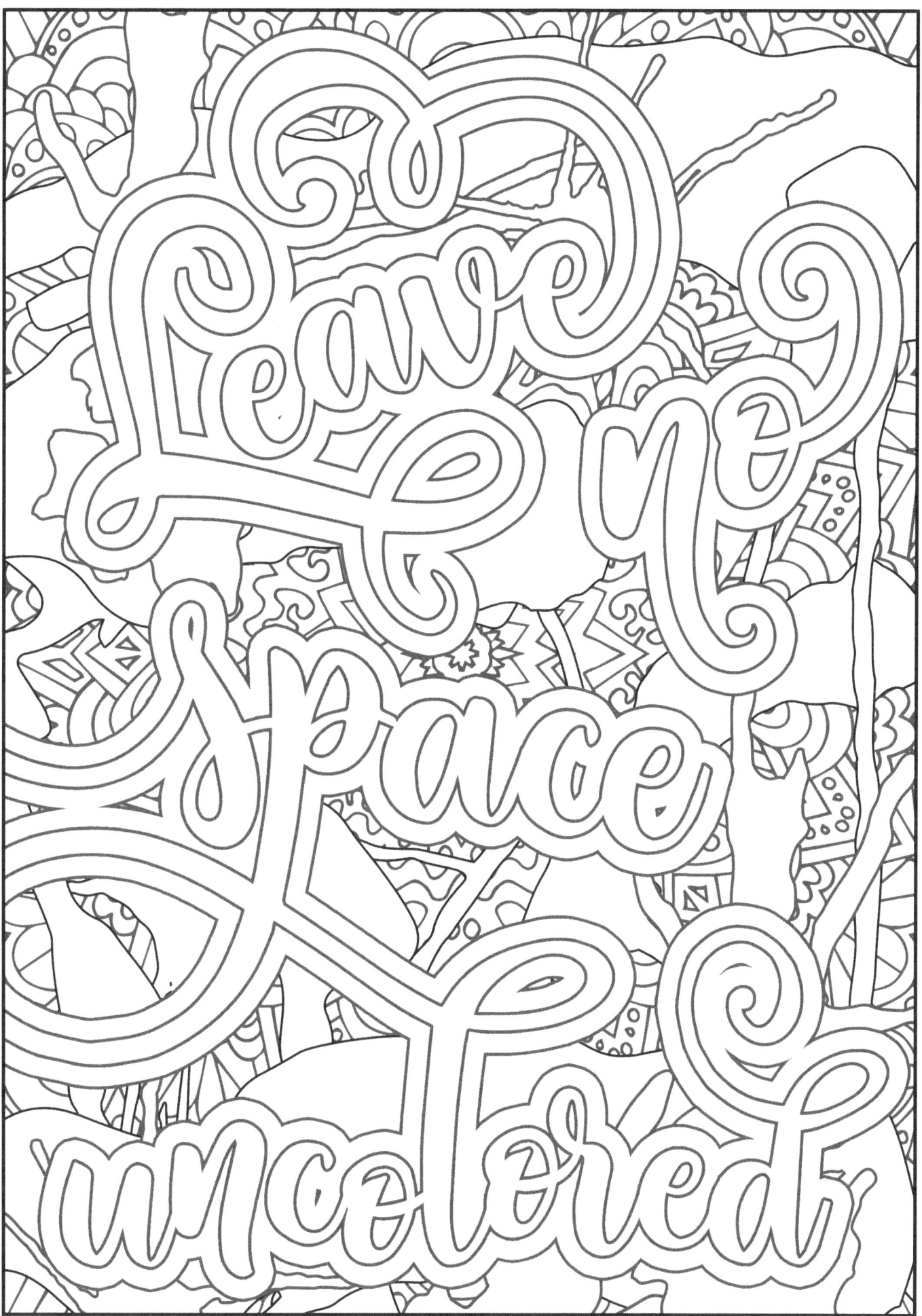

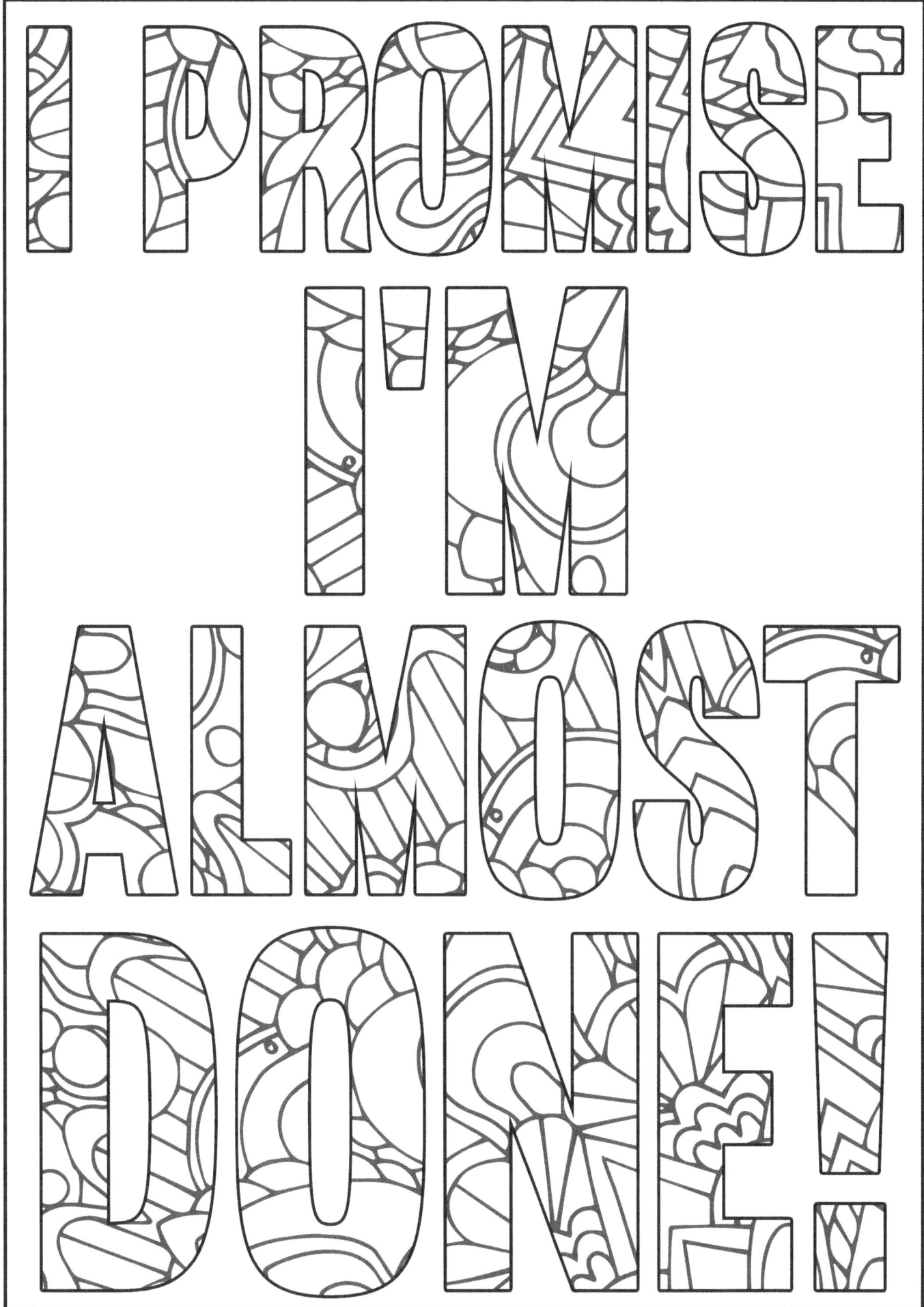

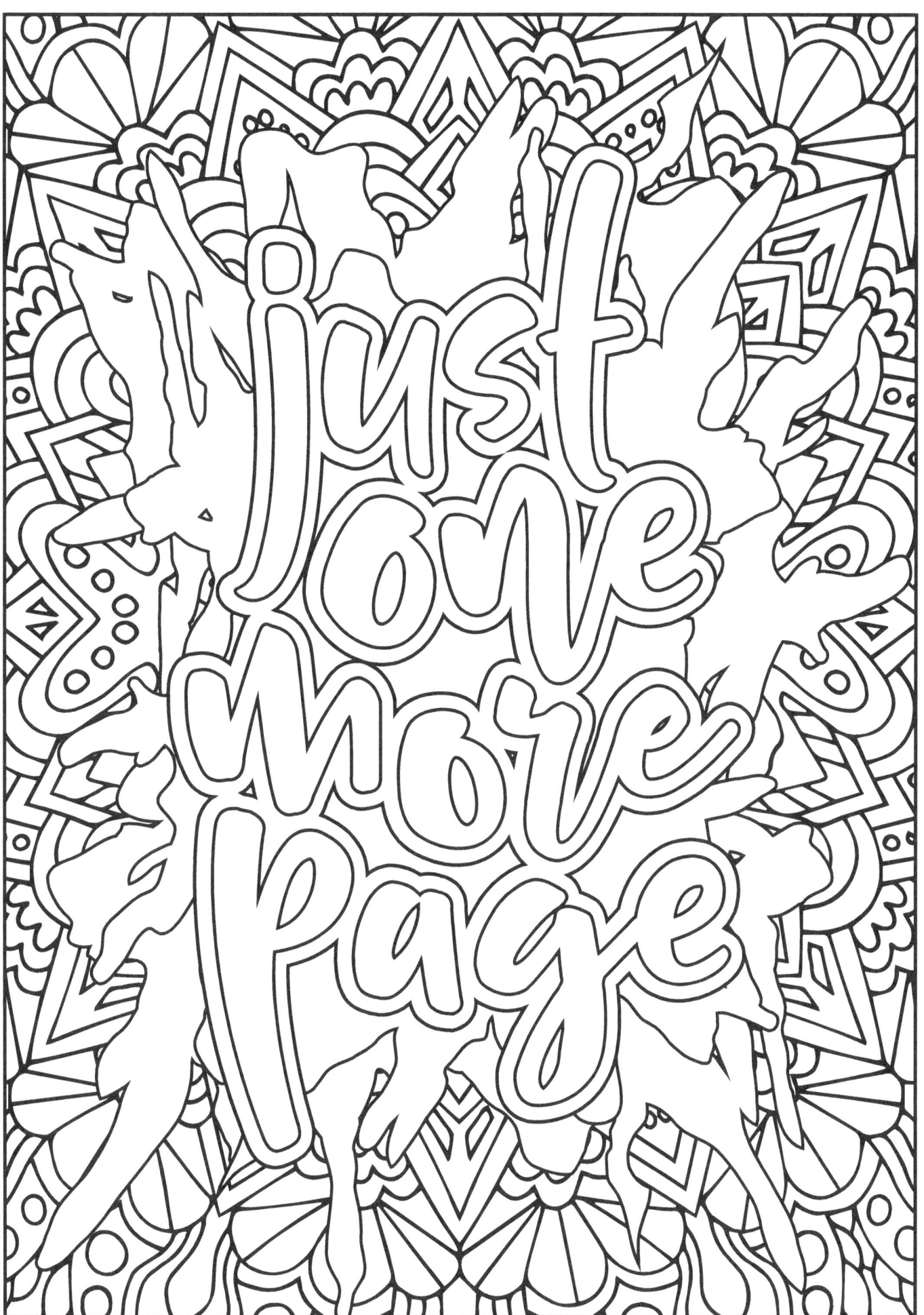

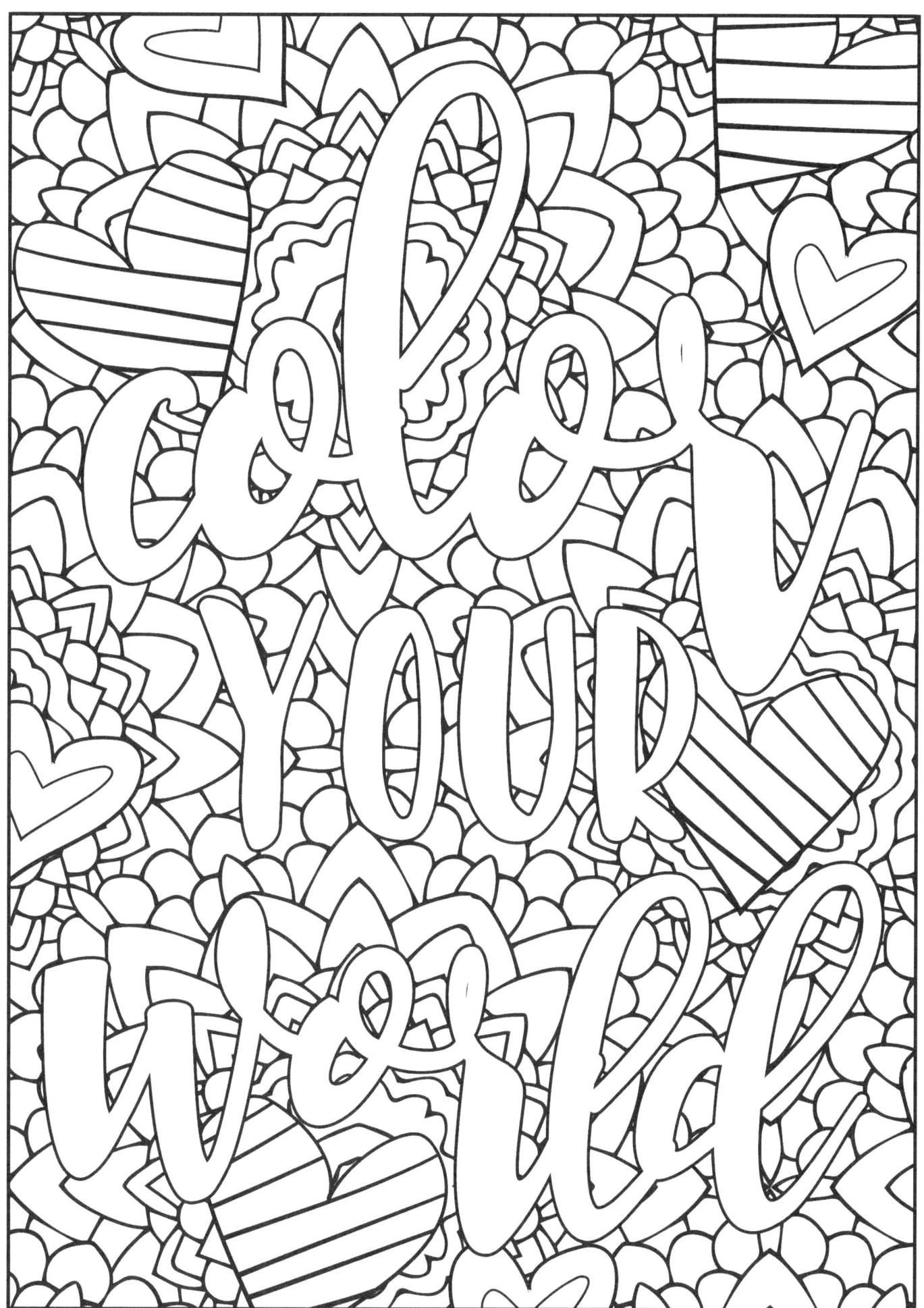

USE THIS COLOR WHEEL TO COMPARE COLORS AND SHADES!

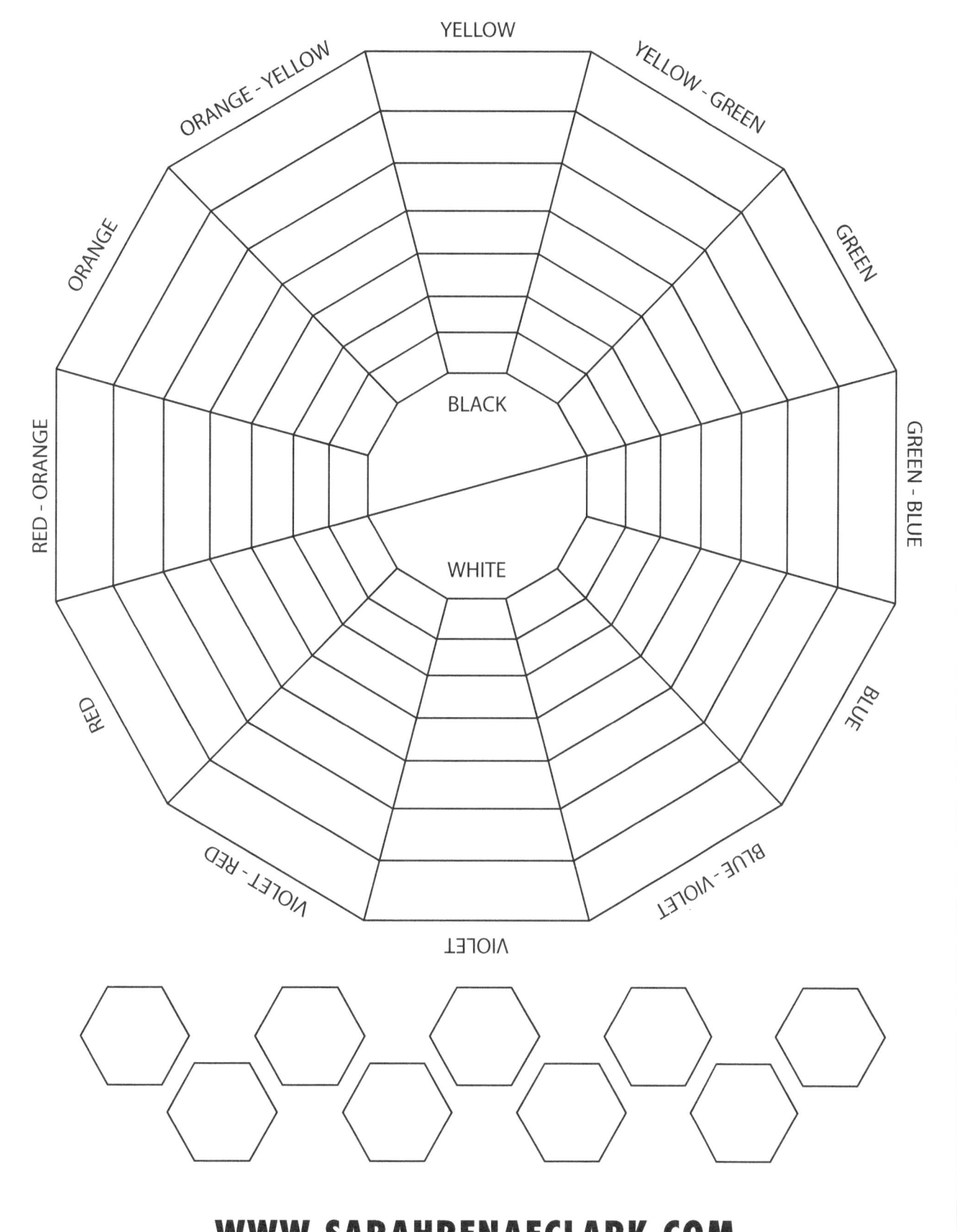

SO, WHAT WILL YOU COLOR NEXT?

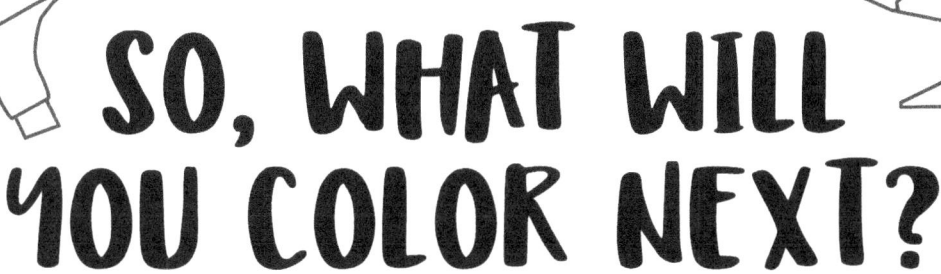

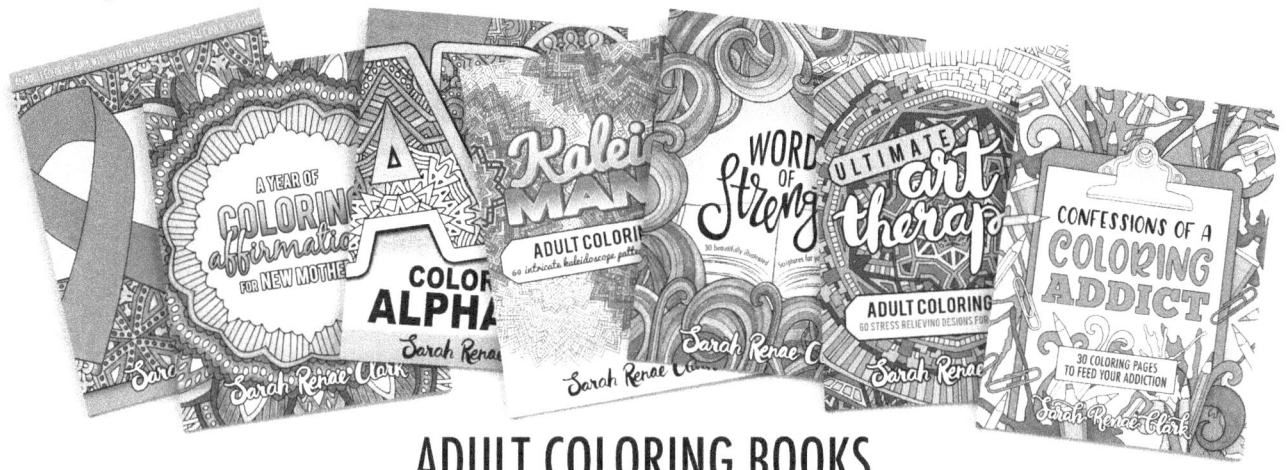

ADULT COLORING BOOKS

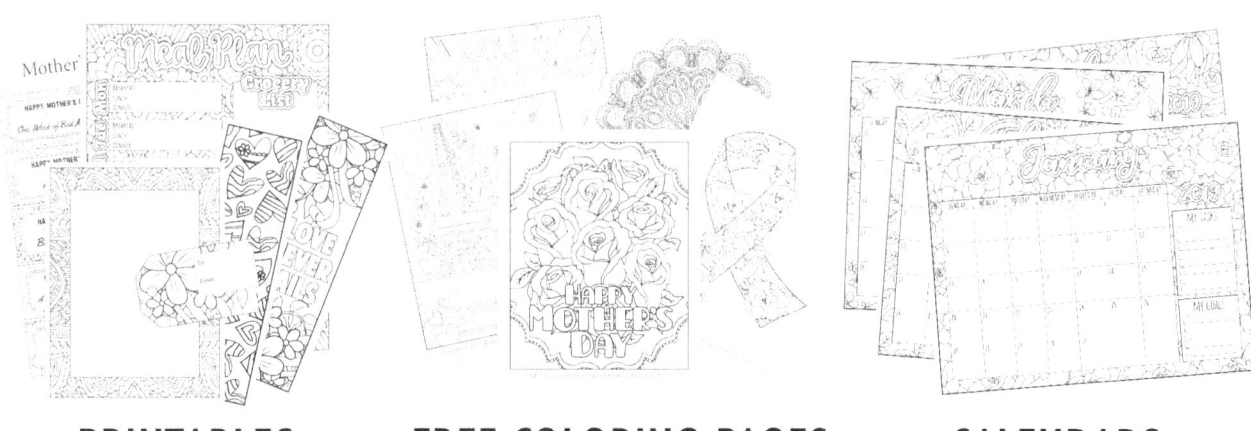

PRINTABLES   FREE COLORING PAGES   CALENDARS

PLUS COLOR PALETTES, COLORING TUTORIALS,
FREE RESOURCES, GIVEAWAYS AND MORE!

CHECK IT ALL OUT AND JOIN THE CLUB
TO GET A FREE COLORING BOOK AT:

SARAHRENAECLARK.COM